Nothing Ever Happens Around Here

Developing Work With Young People in Rural Areas

Dave Phillips and Alison Skinner

YOUTH • WORK • PRESS

Printed and published by Youth Work Press,
17–23 Albion Street, Leicester LE1 6GD.

ISBN 086155 154 0

£9.95

© September 1994

Y O U T H · W O R K · P R E S S
is a publishing imprint of the National Youth Agency

Contents

Foreword

I have a strong personal interest and involvement in youth work, both locally in Lancashire where I live, and as patron of Youth Clubs UK's 80th Anniversary Appeal.

I am pleased, therefore, that the Rural Development Commission has helped to fund the National Youth Agency's three-year rural project as part of our work to improve knowledge of the problems and needs of particular groups of people who face extra difficulties by living in a rural area.

It began in 1990 and was designed to promote and develop aspects of youth work vitally important to overcoming disadvantage experienced by young people living in the countryside.

The NYA team has worked with young people aged 11 to 25 years, concentrating particularly on the 13 to 19-year-old age group. It has confirmed that young people in rural areas do not necessarily have a better quality of life than those who live in cities and towns. They are subject to a quite different set of pressures which can affect their future,

such as fewer and more scattered services with poor access by public transport; restricted opportunities for further education, training and employment; lack of access to low-cost housing for those wishing to leave home; and many suffer from a feeling of loneliness and isolation.

This book explains the history of rural youth work and the development of local authority and voluntary sector policy, establishes a framework of needs and explores different ideas and approaches to youth work, including current examples of good practice. I am sure it will prove to be valuable for both policy makers and youth workers alike.

Lord Shuttleworth
Chairman
Rural Development Commission

Preface

This work springs from a project based at the National Youth Agency (NYA)* between 1990 and 1993. The Youth Work in Rural Areas project was funded by the Rural Development Commission (RDC) with the specific brief to promote youth work that would tackle rural disadvantage. The work used a combination of approaches – undertaking fieldwork, bringing together practitioners and managers for conferences and training events, and desk-based research.

This publication, therefore, draws ideas from a number of sources, hopefully filling a gap among previously published materials concerning youth work and the particular circumstances, experiences and needs of young people who find themselves living in rural locations where, from many young people's perspective, 'nothing ever happens around here …'.

We hope this publication addresses that sense of under-stimulation and enables a range of organisations and individuals to become more creative in developing work with young people in rural areas that highlights the issues and is effective in its outcomes.

Acknowledgments

Throughout the life of the project at the NYA the expertise of rural youth work practitioners and managers was harnessed via a small reference group. This group met nine times between 1990 and 1993, contributing ideas and giving direction and moral support.

In addition, a number of other individuals acted as readers to the first draft of the text. The authors would like to thank all those who contributed, including many who may not realise their contribution – a comment, a dilemma or an idea shared at a conference or recorded via a project report all helped.

Particular mention must also be made of the contribution of Sue Foreman, worker on the project from December 1991 to May 1993.

(* National Youth Bureau until March 1991)

Dave Phillips and **Alison Skinner**

1

Introduction

This publication aims to be an accessible and authoritative source of information, and offer ideas on approaches to work with young people in rural areas. Its aims are to encourage existing policymakers and practitioners to examine their assumptions and practice, and help to spark interest in work with young people among organisations and individuals where the potential benefits of youth work approaches are currently unrecognised or undervalued.

The term 'young people' here refers to those young women and young men who are engaged in the transition to adulthood in the age range 11 to 25, with a particular focus on the 13 to 19 age group.

Youth work as a form of practice will be considered in terms of the Statement of Purpose agreed at the Second Ministerial Conference on the Youth Service held in Birmingham in November 1990 (64). This event, and the consultation that led up to it, was an important stage in a process designed to form a common view on the purpose and nature of youth work in England that could be owned and understood by all organisations involved and more clearly understood by the public.

The Statement of Purpose therefore is the most widely accepted current definition of youth work and its curriculum:

> *The purpose of youth work is to redress all forms of inequality and to ensure equality of opportunity for all young people to fulfil their potential as empowered individuals, members of groups and communities and to support young people during the transition to adulthood.*

The statement goes on to describe four key factors that underpin youth work approaches and which, applied *together*, set youth work apart from other forms of education:

> *Youth work offers young people opportunities which are:*
>
> ♦ *educative – enabling young people to gain the skills, knowledge and attitudes needed to identify, advocate and pursue their rights and responsibilities as individuals and as members of groups and communities locally, nationally and internationally;*
>
> ♦ *designed to promote equality of opportunity*
>   • *through the challenging of oppressions, such as racism and sexism, and all those which spring from differences of culture, race, language, sexual identity, gender,*

disability, age, religion and class;

- *through the celebration of the diversity and strengths which arise from those differences;*

♦ **participative** – *through a voluntary relationship with young people in which young people are partners in the learning process and decision-making structures which affect their own and other young people's lives and their environment; and*

♦ **empowering** – *supporting young people to understand and act on the personal, social and political issues which affect their lives, the lives of others and the communities of which they are a part.*

The three ministerial conferences that took place between 1989 and 1992 also addressed the importance of partnership between the various organisations that work with young people, priorities in terms of age ranges and issues and styles of provision, and worked on developing ways to plan youth work more systematically, to evaluate its effectiveness and to describe its outcomes in ways that would help underline its uniqueness.

At the second ministerial conference it was stated that:

> *Youth work is delivered through a partnership between voluntary organisations and local authorities which provide or facilitate:*
>
> ♦ **informal educational programmes** *which challenge young people and enhance their personal and spiritual development, social and political education;*
>
> ♦ **places and relationships** *within which young people can have fun, feel secure and valued, learn to take control of their lives and to resist the damaging influences which affect them;*
>
> ♦ *access to and ability to use* **relevant information, advice and counselling***;*
>
> ♦ **responsiveness** *by other services to the needs of young people; and*
>
> ♦ **research, monitoring and publication** *of social trends and legislation which affect young people.*

In focusing on young people in rural areas, the term 'work with young people in rural areas' is used to acknowledge that a wide range of groups, organisations and individuals are engaged in youth work using a variety of methods and in many different settings – in villages, rural isolated settlements and hamlets, coastal areas with a rural hinterland, depressed former industrial areas or in edge of town communities that display rural characteristics.

Work with young people in rural areas is undertaken by a wide range of people – some will be full-time employees of local authorities or the staff of national voluntary organisations or local projects. Many more will be giving their time to organisations, interagency groups, local churches and community projects of all kinds as volunteers. The term 'youth worker' therefore will refer to all those who take on the task of working with young people in a strategic way – whether they are unpaid volunteers, sessional workers or full-time staff, and whether or not their organisation explicitly describes itself as an organisation undertaking youth work.

In any particular location, local factors will determine how it is possible to respond to young people's needs. Approaches that are appropriate to rural settings include:

♦ local activities in peer groups and with adults;

♦ area activities;

♦ one night a week clubs;

♦ detached work;

♦ district/patch projects;

♦ distance initiatives using radio and telephone services; and

♦ outreach work and the use of mobile provision to bring facilities into isolated communities.

In many respects work with young people in rural areas is an underdeveloped area of youth work practice. Similarly the needs of rural communities per se are often neglected in the face of preoccupations with urban living and urban ills. There is a widely held assumption that living in rural areas and in small communities automatically confers a better quality of life than existence in decaying inner cities and estates. These and other issues undermine the collective capacity of organisations and individuals to respond to the needs of young people living in rural areas and form part of the rationale for producing this publication.

For some young people there can be very positive benefits associated with growing up in the countryside. Young people can experience a sense of security from longstanding relationships and familiar surroundings and develop a very strong attachment to a place. It is not, therefore, intended in this work to deny any of the potential advantages of rural life.

It is the case, however, that many adults living in rural areas and members of the wider public will overlook the reality that some of the social and physical characteristics of rural living can affect young people in adverse ways that do not apply to adults. Some of these effects are cumulative yet not immediately noticeable. This book aims to alert youth workers and other interested individuals to the range of potential disadvantages young people may experience, show how those experiences can interact with each other in damaging ways and provide pointers to how responses can be directed in a purposeful way when the need becomes apparent.

Some of the inherent features of rural living we identify which may impinge directly on the life opportunities and experiences of young people are:

♦ small population groupings isolated from each other;
♦ poor public transport;
♦ fewer and more scattered public services;
♦ intense relationships between individuals extending over long periods of time;
♦ restricted range of social and economic opportunities;
♦ inertia in social attitudes which may inhibit personal development and preparation for independence;
♦ little social diversity among the local population;
♦ age imbalances;
♦ limited social, leisure and sport facilities;
♦ limited local job prospects; and

♦ limited access to affordable housing.

Many young people growing up in rural areas will be inconvenienced or disadvantaged in some way in comparison with their urban peers. Those who do not have families with sufficient wealth and social and physical mobility to transcend these difficulties face severe restrictions on their leisure, housing and employment opportunities. They may also experience a greater degree of surveillance and supervision from adults than their urban peers and a high degree of unrealised potential, because of a combination of limited horizons, lack of stimulation and few chances for growth and experimentation. Youth work practice in rural areas, therefore, has to be innovative to counter these factors, and at the same time make best use of what are likely to be particularly limited resources.

The chapters that follow examine these themes in greater depth, concluding with a series of recommendations that form a blueprint for action.

2 The Project at the NYA
An overview of the development of the Rural Development Commission-funded work at the NYA from 1990 to 1993, and an examination of the ideas that inform this publication that have been gathered via events and fieldwork.

3 The Context for Rural Youth Work
Definitions of rural life and an examination of the evolution and development of work with young people in rural areas through published literature, recorded practice and the development of networks and campaign groups.

4 Youth Work in the 1990s – Responding to Young People's Needs
Key features of youth work in the 1990s, the needs and difficulties experienced by young people in rural areas, and factors affecting rural youth work responses to them.

5 A Framework of Needs and Responses
Listing of key needs and appropriate youth work responses, with snapshot examples of

contemporary practice. Needs and responses are grouped together under three headings: isolation; identity; and access.

6   Factors Affecting Future Delivery

Current issues in the political environment affecting the delivery of youth work in all settings and their impact on work in rural areas, now and into the future.

7   Conclusions

Implications from the practice observed and recorded throughout the project, highlighting features of good practice with recommendations for strategies which will support and enhance future work.

Appendices

Target Audience

The readership for this publication might include the following:

- sponsors of work with young people in rural areas;
- funders of rural youth work;
- elected members of all kinds;
- specialist rural workers;
- youth work students;
- youth work managers; and
- full-time and part-time youth workers in rural areas.

Each are likely to be interested in different aspects of the work and it is not anticipated that people will necessarily be reading the document in its entirety. Chapter 5 in particular is viewed as a resource for people to use in relation to their own practice. The chapter headings and indexes will lead readers to the work of most benefit to them, whether it be specific examples of practice or ideas for training and policy development of direct relevance to managers.

The descriptions of practice are relevant to England only as this was the target area for the project. It is hoped, however, that potential readers elsewhere – particularly in Wales, Scotland and Northern Ireland – will find some insights relevant to their experience, although it is acknowledged that each will have their own distinctive cultural and geographical perspectives on the issues we raise.

The three-year project focusing on the needs of young people in rural areas was a welcome innovation on the part of the RDC which enabled a considerable amount of disparate and long-standing practice to be recorded in a systematic and coherent fashion. It is hoped that this record of the process will provide an acceptable distillation of the expertise of the many people who have dedicated their working lives to rural issues and to young people growing up in rural situations.

2

The Project at the NYA

Throughout the 1980s, the then National Youth Bureau (NYB), sought to provide resources and support to the development of youth work in rural areas via its established range of services. These included *Shadows of Adolescence* (1984) ([45]), articles in *Youth in Society* and *Youth Service Scene* ([94]), the provision of information through the Bureau's Information Services Team and developmental work through the Field Services Team and its youth work advisers.

Work alongside rural practitioners and officers, including the emerging Rural Youth Work Network, meant involvement in the three national symposia that took place between 1985 and 1987 – in Buckinghamshire ([18]), Lancashire ([63]) and Taunton ([87]) – and in the work of the National Advisory Council for the Youth Service (NACYS) Subcommittee which produced the report *Youth Work in Rural Areas* in March 1988 ([56]).

By the late 1980s it was clearly time for a systematic examination of the developments in rural work that had been taking place. A focus could then be given to rural work within the emerging debate about the curriculum, organisation and delivery of youth work prompted by the promised series of ministerial conferences and the acceleration of legislative challenge affecting education and its relationships with local government.

In 1988 the fusion between the former Development Commission and the Council for Small Industries in Rural Areas (CoSIRA) created the Rural Development Commission (RDC), a single national agency with responsibility for promoting both economic and social aspects of rural life. The RDC became an obvious potential partner for work focusing on the experience and contribution of young people to life in rural areas. The announcement of the RDC's Social Partnership Fund in December 1989 led to a formal bid from the NYB in May 1990 for a project designed to 'promote and develop aspects of youth work vitally important in combating disadvantage experienced by young people living in rural areas'.

The bid set out some of the disadvantages already known to be experienced by young people living in rural areas, the potential of youth work to address these needs, and it outlined a range of objectives:

- identify a range of appropriate models for youth work practice;
- outline patterns of effective management and delivery;
- promote appropriate training;
- raise the profile of rural work via reports and articles;
- support the (then new) national forum for youth work in rural areas; and
- ensure a rural dimension to national debates concerning youth work.

In 1990, the youth service was entering a phase in which many organisations would be restructured and reorganised. The context of the project, therefore, was one of considerable change from which the host organisation itself was not immune – NYB becoming the National Youth Agency (NYA) in 1991.

Evolution

Project approval in September 1990 enabled the NYA to make an immediate start on the work using the spring-board of the training event Innovations in Rural Practice (London, October 1990) which brought together practitioners either new to rural work or working in newly-created posts.

The need for an external reference group to help shape the work of the project was quickly identified. This group first met formally in February 1991 and continued to meet on a quarterly basis throughout the life of the three-year project. Membership was targeted to draw on the experiences of practitioners and managers from all sectors of the youth service and from different parts of the country. (For a list of reference group members, see Appendix IV, page 113.)

Work on the project developed in two distinct phases.

Phase I from September 1990 to September 1991 involved four main strands of work:

- mapping the range of current practice with young people in rural areas – particularly identifying innovation and development;
- the publication of descriptive accounts of interesting practice – see *Working with Rural Youth*, Peter White/Youth Work Press, October 1991 (99);
- supporting the development of appropriate policy and management approaches; and
- supporting the national Rural Youth Work Network.

Phase II occupied the two-year period between October 1991 and September 1993. Building on the work of Phase I, an ambitious programme of work was set out designed to:

- influence thinking around developments in youth service curriculum planning and evaluation techniques relevant to work in rural settings;
- identify good practice in response to a range of curriculum issues – housing need and homelessness, the need for positive images of rural lives, tackling discrimination and racism, working with young parents, the use of arts as a medium, access to vocational training, and the use of mobiles, e.g. buses, vans and caravans, to take facilities to isolated communities;
- promote work in rural areas through networks and forums, published articles, involvement in events, and to offer an information and enquiry service;
- provide support to organisations working with young people in rural areas through periods of change prompted by legislation, reorganisation or review; and
- develop appropriate training approaches.

The themes addressed a range of contemporary issues affecting all youth work but each had a specific rural dimension. The programme of work therefore, while free-standing, was also tailored to integrate with, and capitalise on, the wider work of the Agency – able to draw on expertise located elsewhere in the organisation and on opportunities to access and influence other items of work.

Staffing for the first phase of the project was drawn from the existing establishment of NYB with a commission for the first publication. A specialist post was created within the Curriculum Development Team of the newly-created NYA for Phase II.

Throughout the project, staff from a number of the Agency's teams were also involved – from the Organisation Development, Information Services and Training Development teams.

In the event, some of the planned themes were explored more fully than others. Interest in some topics grew beyond our expectations while others were more difficult to engage in from a single, national vantage point. All the themes originally highlighted find their place in this publication but unfortunately we cannot be sure that we identified all the practice.

3

The Context for Rural Youth Work

3A
Defining Rurality

I climbed through great beechwoods which seemed in the twilight like some green place far below the sea and then over a short stretch of hill pasture to the rim of the vale. All about me were little fields enclosed with walls of grey stone and full of dim sheep. I could see the stream slipping among its water-meadows and could hear the splash of the weir. A tiny village settled in the crook of the hill and its church tower sounded seven with a curious sweet chime.

John Buchan, *Mr Standfast* (Penguin)

Black fen they call it round here. Black for the dark peaty soil. Flat, flat land, extending as far as the eye can see with no distinguishing characteristics which for a stranger would separate one, monotonous stretch from another. Hedges and trees are fast disappearing, creating for the farmer a few more valuable feet per acre but also encouraging the wind, which needs no additional incentive here ... Life on the land is neither romantic nor glamorous. Just hard work, in uncompromising weather, in rough old working clothes, padded out with newspaper against the wind.

Mary Chamberlain, *Fenwomen* (Virago, 1975)

I had thought travelling round Britain would be a breeze; without a car it was often very difficult. It revealed to me long coastal stretches of unexpected decrepitude ... it was another area of disused railway lines. Trains are different from country to country, but buses are pretty much the same the world over. I stood in a long line of people at the bus shelter – no-one knew when the bus was due – and waited for an hour or more on a windy road, and then I saw the bus moving slowly down a road five hills away and I crowded in and bounced for another hour to go fifteen miles; and I thought Afghanistan. It was like travelling in a Third World Country.

Paul Theroux, *The Kingdom by the Sea* (Penguin, 1983)

There are contradictions inherent in any examination of the nature of the countryside and of rural life. They highlight the contrast between the widely held view of the countryside which many people believe to be their national heritage and the actual place where real people have to exist and make a living and where young people have to grow up and make sense of the world.

John Buchan captures the romantic vision of the southern downland countryside. It is a landscape which still exists (just), and in which many people aspire to live, and to preserve.

In the second extract Mary Chamberlain describes a setting which although specific to the fens applies to many areas where agriculture remains an economic way of life. People make a living there. It does not conform to orthodox standards of aesthetic beauty and tends not to attract many people to settle who are not directly involved in farming.

Finally, Paul Theroux underlines the way in which so many basic services have been withdrawn from vast areas of the country, leaving those without personal transport to manage as best they can with intermittent public transport.

Howard Newby, *Green and Pleasant Land?* ([65]) describes the process by which our vision of the countryside has been fashioned.

The eighteenth century landowner, through the agency of his hired landscapers, invented what we have now come to accept as picturesque natural beauty. Nature was re-arranged to comply with pictorial design and this contrivance has henceforth provided a standard by which all landscapes have been judged. The eighteenth century thus provided a decisive break between the ideas of nature and beauty on the one hand and a functional countryside on the other – a divergence which has remained until the present day ... In the eighteenth century a new commercial rural economy was being created, but all this was separated and hidden away ... Those who actually worked on the land became mere figures in a landscape, granted an aesthetic identity, but denied any personal or social existence. Perhaps it is no coincidence that areas formally designated as being of 'outstanding natural beauty' are predominantly located in countryside of low agricultural value ... it is because picturesque landscapes have become, almost by definition, agriculturally marginal and our criteria of English landscape beauty

are taken from a standard which is designed to be outdated and which obscures current realities.

As Newby has identified there is a fundamental conflict between the type of landscape valued by a predominantly urban population for its recreational purposes/spiritual uplift and that required by modern economic farming and industrial development.

With the current disillusion with urban inner-city living, the preservation of the countryside has become important to many more people. By and large, however, it is the parts of the countryside which conform to the romantic vision of the urban population which have received the most attention and attracted new recruits to rural life. The marginal industrial and coastal areas have been left to decay and their decline is accelerating in the wake of the steep industrial decline of the last few decades.

The report *Faith in the Countryside* commissioned by the Church of England (1990) ([1]) notes:

The countryside still seems reassuringly stable, a refuge from the thrust of technology and the tough realities of work and competition in the cities ... (but) the truth is that social and economic forces often with a national or international impetus, are transforming rural England. In the 1980s, such processes accelerated – varied and uneven in their occurrence, but far reaching in their impacts.

Almost every aspect of rural life has altered significantly since the Second World War. There have been substantial shifts in the structure of the rural population, traumatic changes to the patterns of agricultural production, new problems associated with the emergence of a changed working base for the rural economy, and social transformations arising from the movement of growing numbers of professional people out of the cities into rural areas. Not surprisingly, the consequence of such change has been increasing tensions in rural life.

These tensions are reflected in new questions that are now being asked of the countryside.

Should the rural areas be developed only in ways consistent with traditional patterns of employment – or in ways less inhibited by the past? What sorts of rural communities should be encouraged in the last part of the 20th century, and with what mixes of population? Who 'owns' the countryside, and what rights and obligations should such 'ownership' entail? What priority should be given to nature as opposed to people? Whose interests should come first – those of established rural dwellers, or those escaping from conurbations to new forms of living?

Rural Definitions

There are no universally accepted definitions of rural life and many of those which do exist are based on characteristics of urban life from which the rural situation is assumed to deviate. Land is frequently deemed to be rural if it has not been classified as urban.

The National Council for Voluntary Organisation's (NCVO) paper *Getting Closer to Rural Communities* by Liz Barnes (1993) [10] provides a useful overview of the different definitions of rurality currently in use. She asserts the importance of using definitions of rurality appropriate to the intended purpose:

> *Most definitions are devised for a particular purpose. Used out of context they can lead to misguided policies. What is important is to find an approach that works for your organisation, bringing you closer to those who are missing out ...*

By exploring a range of currently used rural definitions – the Office of Population Censuses and Surveys urban/non-urban definition, population density, electoral ward categorisation and other socio-economic clarifications – Barnes provides a composite set of (some) rural characteristics.

Population

♦ Smaller percentage of population born outside UK;

♦ sparse and scattered population with small settlements;

♦ percentage of pensioners exceeds the national average; and

♦ higher rates of cars per household.

Physical Characteristics

♦ Distant from large towns – remote from main cities; and

♦ landscape and weather affect daily life and communications.

Economic Activity

♦ Limited work, training, cultural and social opportunities;

♦ higher percentage of people work in agriculture, forestry and fishing;

♦ more people work from home – most commuters depend on cars; and

♦ rural wages lower than the national average.

Services

♦ Limited local services and poor public transport; and

♦ difficulties of access to central services and information.

Housing

♦ Lower percentage of council and housing association homes;

♦ high percentage of owner occupiers, high house prices;

♦ higher percentage of privately-rented unfurnished homes, tied accommodation and homes in poor condition; and

♦ higher percentage of large, often under occupied homes.

Rural Services

According to the RDC, ten million people – one-fifth of the population – live and work in rural England. The RDC also publishes statistics on rural conditions (1993) [76].

The Rural Economy

In a number of respects the condition of rural England is improving. From 1981–91 the population of remoter rural districts rose by 6.4 per cent; between 1981–89 high technology industries grew by 12 per cent in rural counties and fell by 16 per cent in urban areas; and from 1989–91 employment in a sample of firms in remote rural areas increased by four employees on average and fell by 1.6 employees in urban areas.

However, unemployment in the rural areas has been increasing and is above the national average in some cases. Added to this are limited job prospects and difficult access to training. Although agriculture remains the largest industry, it employs only 2 per cent of England's workforce and is declining fast. Published estimates suggest that up to 100,000 full-time jobs in UK farming may disappear during this decade, with up to 55,000 jobs in related industries by 1995. The extractive industries, such as coal, tin and china clay are also experiencing decline with over 37,000 rural coal mining jobs lost between 1984 and 1991.

The Shortage of Affordable Housing

This is a critical problem. The influx of more affluent long-distance commuters and second-home owners is reducing the availability of affordable property and is forcing young, local families to move away, depriving rural areas of their skills and adding to urban pressures. An estimated 80,000 affordable homes are needed in rural areas in the next four years.

Declining Village Services

The decline in village services brings increased difficulty of access to shops, schools and healthcare, causing particular problems where public transport is limited and expensive.

In 1991, a survey carried out for the Commission found that 39 per cent of parishes had no shop, 40 per cent no post office, 51 per cent no school, 29 per cent no village hall and 73 per cent no daily bus service. [76]

The RDC's own criteria for the designation of its priority Rural Development Areas (RDAs) are also worth noting:

♦ persistent high unemployment;
♦ low male and/or female activity rates, low pay and seasonality of employment;
♦ a narrow industrial and employment structure resulting in over dependence on a few sources of employment, limited job choice, etc;
♦ the decline or disappearance of local services and the difficulties of access by those who are less mobile or without access by car to services provided increasingly in larger centres; and
♦ the disadvantage experienced by some individuals or groups within small communities, particularly as a result of their location in rural areas (e.g. elderly people, the young, people with disabilities, those in need of care and carers and women – especially those with young children).

From another perspective, James Garo Derounian's *Another Country: Real Life Beyond Rose Cottage* (1993) [23] provides a detailed overview of current living conditions in rural areas. Derounian asserts the extent of rural deprivation and quotes research suggesting that there are two million disadvantaged people in rural England – suffering low wages, poor personal mobility, poor access to housing and the absence of a range of other basic services.

The implications for young people are not uniform. There are very considerable social, economic and physical variations between different types of rural areas and different regions of the country, for example. Young people will share many of the potential problems common to all rural dwellers such as isolation and mobility difficulties, but the social context for each may be very different. Some will live in beautiful scenic areas where there is an optimistic view of the economic future, others will come from dreary wastelands where economic activity is declining and future prospects are grim. Some will be willing participants in rural life while others may be desperate to escape.

Many sons and daughters of rural incomers may not share their parents' choice to move into a rural situation and even if they shared the theory, the reality may not meet expectations. What is important, therefore, is to understand the significance of rural factors on the lives of individual young people whether local or incomer. Whatever the impact of rural disadvantage on adults, the effects on young people will be compounded by both structural and cultural factors which exclude young people from influencing most matters that affect them and by young people's perceptions of their own situation.

Types of Rural Location

Because differing locations and types of settlement of rural England present their own individual characteristics, youth work needs to assume specific styles to match particular circumstances. While many rural situations defy easy categorisation, a series of profiles is presented here to assist the development of youth work responses:

♦ remote rural areas;
♦ villages;
♦ market towns;
♦ collapsed industrial areas; and
♦ coastal areas and hinterland.

Remote Rural Areas

Isolated farms, single dwellings and scattered settlements are characteristic of the more remote rural parts of the country including the uplands of North Yorkshire, parts of the Southwest, the Welsh marches, Cumbria, Northumbria and the fenland of East Anglia. The social characteristics of communities in these areas include:

♦ more difficult access to basic services;
♦ fewer resources such as general meeting halls;
♦ high or nil tourist/visitor presence;
♦ poor housing;

♦ rural poverty;
♦ little collective political influence;
♦ strong farming culture;
♦ strong local identities and traditions with scope for positive attachments by young people;
♦ smaller pools of potential volunteers to support youth work than in some other rural areas;
♦ social attitudes that might limit relationships and career options;
♦ long journeys to school; and
♦ extreme isolation for many young people and little or no peer culture.

Satisfactory youth work responses in such settings take the form of sustained efforts to contact young people, to bring them together, provide personal support and offer access to wider experiences.

Villages

Different types of villages are found throughout the countryside. From a youth work point of view, three basic types can be distinguished by a combination of their location, characteristics and varying potential for youth work (there will inevitably be some overlap in these characteristics between villages – they are offered only as useful models).

Commuter/Dormitory

These are villages located close to urban settlements which may have difficulty in establishing their own identity and thus miss the attention given to others. Some of their characteristics include:

♦ uncommitted incomers;
♦ local services nearer but access still difficult for those without personal transport;
♦ difficulty in recruiting local adults prepared to become involved in youth work;
♦ few local resources such as halls and leisure amenities; and
♦ contrasts of wealth and poverty with some incomers having access to the best of both rural/urban lifestyle and others trapped without access to either.

Appropriate youth work responses might involve outreach from the nearest town which has a good range of youth provision, club-based work or detached work. Resources from a number of organisations may be available – the LEA; voluntary sector organisations – both local and national; district and parish councils; and community associations.

Established/Attractive

These are the villages of long-established settlement which have been experiencing growth and changing character during the past 20 years. Characteristics include:

♦ seasonal visitors with a consequent difficulty for young people living there to assert any real indigenous culture ('goldfish bowl' syndrome);

♦ an expanding population;

♦ a committed incomer culture with two possible outcomes: either
  • increased pool of volunteers/skills to draw on; or
  • a NIMBY (Not In My Back Yard) syndrome of potential hostility to new developments/services;

♦ more resources such as halls and better amenities but which may be too expensive to use for youth work;

♦ access to services and towns more difficult;

♦ variety of differing groupings in the local community with potentially competing interests;

♦ contrasts of wealth and poverty; and

♦ expensive housing.

Youth work responses will depend a great deal on the prevailing attitudes towards young people. There may be the resources to establish a village club and volunteers to support it, but hostility towards young people may lead to difficulties in sustaining provision and in devising a programme that addresses real issues. Alternative strategies are feasible, however, such as outreach work from nearby market towns, networking of provision in different villages, greater reliance on school-based

provision and an emphasis on promoting voluntary youth provision based on established community resources such as church-based groups.

Declining/Under Resourced

These are villages which have not attracted the attention of incomers and have been progressively losing their amenities. Characteristics include:

♦ little positive identity with low attachment on the part of young people;

♦ minimal (and probably decaying) community facilities and resources;

♦ difficult access to outside services;

♦ difficulty in sustaining the village as a social and economic unit as jobs become scarce and fewer people are left to organise community activities;

♦ few volunteers, but those that exist likely to be indigenous;

♦ outward migration of those with the opportunity;

♦ feelings of apathy and depression among those who are left behind; and

♦ people feeling trapped in their surroundings with no choice as to whether they move.

Appropriate youth work responses might take the form of getting young people out to better resourced centres through area networking, or bringing resources into the village with mobile provision and engaging in face-to-face work on young people's own territory.

Market Towns

Market towns will be the largest and best resourced of rural communities in terms of shops and facilities and may have:

♦ a number of young people from outlying areas will assert their identity and sub-culture;

♦ a committed incomer culture with potential of positive or negative outcomes: either
  • the identification of a pool of

volunteers with potential skills and interests to sustain a range of activities; or

- conflict with indigenous community leaders resistant to change;
♦ traditional youth provision but probably of inconsistent quality;
♦ few specialist single issues services;
♦ secondary schools with potential, if not already existing, youth work provision;
♦ a range of leisure facilities but not all accessible to young people;
♦ many needs unidentified and unmet; and
♦ potential conflict between needs of adults and young people.

Satisfactory youth work responses include outreach to outlying areas, inter-agency coordination of existing services and the development of targeted services. Market towns now probably possess the greatest potential for targeted and innovative youth work in the country.

Apart from the deeply rural parts of the country already discussed, there are two other distinctive types of area whose nature and characteristics in themselves will influence the type of youth work that is appropriate and likely to exist: collapsed industrial areas, and coastal areas and hinterland.

Collapsed Industrial Areas

These are areas such as the Durham, East Midlands and Yorkshire coalfields, the china clay workings in Cornwall and many other declining industrial areas with rural characteristics. The typical community is the industrial settlement currently facing very severe economic decline. They are characterised by:

- ♦ high unemployment and dependence on benefits;
- ♦ exploited 'used up' landscapes;
- ♦ feelings of loss of direction and powerlessness among those who have lost their jobs;
- ♦ little sense of a future for those who stay and particularly for young people;

♦ strong indigenous local community and tradition – few incomers;
♦ ambiguous identity on the part of young people – strong ties to local community evident but many young people likely to exhibit ambitions to be elsewhere; and
♦ difficulty in harnessing local effort.

Appropriate youth work responses will be strongly developmental – with a long lead-time. Projects based in the locality with specialist multi-services for local people that encourage wider community vision and involvement are most likely to succeed.

Coastal Areas and Hinterland

Those areas such as parts of the Northeast, Northwest, East Midlands, East Anglia, South and Southwest coasts, formerly prosperous, which have in some cases recently been awarded assisted-area status by the Government under the EEC Atlantic arc scheme, fall into this category. While all coastal areas (particularly resorts) share the experience of seasonal fluctuations in economy, there are considerable differences between the visited and less visited areas. In the former young people will have to compete for resources with visitors at tourist resorts during the season, but those living in run down coastal areas will be in much greater need of services of all kinds all year round. Characteristics include:

- ♦ coastal resorts with large numbers of visitors at particular times of the year;
- ♦ other coastal towns and hinterland with few visitors or attractions;
- ♦ strong seasonal contrasts with facilities available in summer months, closed over the winter;
- ♦ fluctuating local economy and personal income with little control from year to year;
- ♦ undeveloped hinterland reliant on resort-based employment opportunities and social amenities;
- ♦ swamping of resources such as accommodation during the tourist season;
- ♦ different local groupings competing for resources and often mutually antagonistic,

such as local adults and young people, a transient year-round population of retired people and job seekers, seasonal visitors;

♦ young people alternately resentful of, reliant on and in competition with visitors and tourists;

♦ little indigenous industry apart from tourism, with what is still in existence likely to be declining, environmentally unsound or unattractive to many young people, for example, fishing, extractive industries, power generation, refineries, and chemical plants; and

♦ age distributions skewed in some places with negative attitudes to young people likely in places with a high percentage of retired people.

Good youth workers will be alert to the seasonal variations in the needs and interests of local young people and to recognise that young people's responsibilities may be stretched to include working with visitors. Appropriate youth work provision may be in the form of cafes and targeted services, such as information and advice on drugs misuse, wider health issues and youth accommodation.

3B
Key Published Documents on Work With Young People in Rural Areas 1944–90

Existing literature on work with young people in rural areas records the struggle of rural youth workers to gain recognition of the special nature of rural work and the resources to meet the needs of young people living there. Workers who opt for rural youth work, either as a result of their background or interest, will always be aware of the underlying message from the profession – towns and cities are where the real action takes place. A positive outcome of the last ten years is that attitudes such as these are breaking down and parity of esteem for youth work in rural areas is gradually being achieved.

Available literature documents the growing acceptance of the significance of rural youth work in official publications and the increasing substance and relevance of statements made about the purpose and direction of the work. The record of practice also develops from isolated descriptions of individual projects, to a more systematic record of methods and approaches, albeit with little analysis of the implications of such accounts.

Pioneers and Official Sources

The most definitive recent publication on work with young people in rural areas – the occasional paper of the same title by Ray Fabes and Cherie Knowles [32] – has provided a useful overview of the early literature on work in rural areas. Much of the earliest documentation comes from the major voluntary youth organisations, but even this is less complete than might be expected.

Two significant documents from the end of the Second World War start to make the case for a distinctive kind of youth work in rural areas. Désirée Edwards-Rees [30], later to become a member of Her Majesty's Inspectorate (HMI), writing in 1944 noted that the crusaders of the youth service went out into city slums and that:

The more the social conscience of the nation quickened on behalf of the cities, the more it seems to have slumbered in the assurance that if all was not materially well in the country, at least eternal values were safe there.

She documents the familiar difficulty of the small village club without transport and resources, the need for encouragement of volunteers from the local community to share their interests and skills, the different kinds of rural communities which are developing and the needs of young men and women living in rural areas to have their horizons widened, and she called for more sensitive responses to the developing needs of countryside dwellers and a redressing of previous neglect. In a chapter on the work of the country youth leader she makes a telling point:

> Above all it will be useless if rural youth workers are to regard their country jobs as avenues of promotion to town work. Nor should they look at the country through the rose-coloured spectacles of country holiday-making. Unless they know and understand it, and care for its people as country people they had better not undertake the work at all.

Another pioneer, Edith M. Clark ([15]), published a book entitled *Youth and the Village Club* in 1946. This went into greater detail concerning the nature of village youth club work in Scotland and presented what amounted to a systematic curriculum, starting with local knowledge and resources to foster interest in a wide range of subjects. She notes in her introduction that:

> Youth service is no longer a preventive measure. It is acknowledged as an important means of civic training and, as such, it is as much the right of the boy and girl of the farm and country home as of those who work in factories and offices.

The book addresses the questions of where to meet, what to do, and who is to lead – issues which still exercise rural youth workers today. The overall aim of youth work, she asserts, is 'to develop in youth a sense of purpose, joy and adventure in living'.

Following these two works, there appears to have been a long silence from official sources until 1963 when R. D. Salter-Davis ([80]), HMI, chaired a subcommittee of the Youth Service Development Council. The Council had been set up as one of the recommendations of the Albemarle Report ([7]) of 1960, which itself had made no reference at all to youth work in rural areas. The subcommittee produced a report entitled *The Problems of Youth Work in Rural Areas* which reviewed the issues and some contemporary youth work responses to them.

It made some far-sighted recommendations for the youth service in rural areas, urging it to become more flexible and diversified than the service in the towns and even more ready to use unconventional methods. It called for more training and information, more experimentation in converting existing premises for youth work, including lofts, disused barns, oasthouses and redundant schools. It was also prophetic in perceiving a value in the use of mobiles:

> Facilities for young people to meet in a way so far tried only in 'drop-in' youth centres in towns might be provided by a peripatetic 'hop-on' vehicle.

The report concluded:

> We believe the profound differences between youth work in the country and in the town will remain … the sociological aspects of rural life, and their effect on the personal development of young people, cannot be ignored.

This report's interest in rural issues proved to be a one-off as the long official silence continued. The Fairbairn/Milson report ([34]) of 1969 *Youth and Community Work in the '70s* made no reference to rural practice at all. Rural youth workers had to wait until the Thompson Report ([90]) of 1982 to receive a clear validation of their work. Even this did not come about without some pressure.

A lobby group of rural youth workers formed the Campaign for Rural Youth (CRY) following an annual meeting of the then National Association of Youth Clubs (NAYC) in 1978. CRY coordinated a lobby of members and contacts to write to the Thompson Committee inviting them to visit rural areas during their enquiry. The paper *Missed the Bus* ([14]), published in 1979 for the Youth Parliamentary Lobby, identified important factors which had simultaneously urbanised and isolated the countryside. They highlighted lack of public transport, disadvantage in education, poverty, housing and inadequate employment opportunities as all having an adverse effect on young people in rural areas.

The Thompson Report [90] devoted five paragraphs to youth work in rural areas and had a considerable influence on subsequent developments in youth service policy. It acknowledged that provision for young people in rural areas was problematic and that the difficulties were exacerbated by little recognition of the issues and inadequate funding. The principle of parity was clearly stated, however:

> Clearly it is difficult to provide a comprehensive youth service in all rural areas. It is important, however, when discussing and seeking solutions to problems of rural deprivation, that the needs of young people are also considered ... The employment of a youth and community worker to work with a variety of age groups, or alternatively a joint teacher/youth work appointment helps the provision of professional support to youth groups in rural areas.

The lack of transport was recognised as a key factor in preventing young people reaching the places where viable youth service provision could be made.

The final paragraph sets out a challenge to the youth service to respond effectively to rural issues:

> The major difficulty that those in rural areas face is that their numbers are small, their difficulties go unnoticed and resources are not provided. Their forms of alienation may be as acute as those in urban areas and may be compounded by their isolation. The solution requires not only a fair share of resources but also appropriate styles of work, support and provision.

Fabes and Knowles [32] observe that these sections of the Thompson Report provided a major stimulus which encouraged those in both statutory and voluntary youth services to begin to pay far greater attention to their involvement in rural areas in England and Wales.

The next major official landmark was the National Advisory Council for the Youth Service (NACYS) report, *Youth Work in Rural Areas*, published in March 1988 [56].

NACYS was created in 1985 to advise ministers on the priority needs of young people and appropriate youth work responses. It set up a number of subcommittees on special areas of youth work – rural work was one of them. Its existence enabled a number of rural practitioners to develop their argument concerning the special nature of work in rural areas.

The NACYS report documented the growing consciousness of rural youth workers as an identifiable group:

> However difficult it is to achieve a working definition of rural youth work, there are many workers, full-time and part-time, paid and voluntary, employed by local education authorities and by voluntary youth organisations who see themselves as 'rural youth workers' and consider that they have many experiences, objectives, problems and aspirations in common. This is demonstrated by the formation of support networks aimed at providing mutual support and pressure groups whose aim is to enhance the quality of rural youth work and make the case for resources. Rural youth workers may sometimes wish to challenge the more simplistic assumptions which are made about the distinctions between the needs of young people in rural settings, not least the assumption that rural youth work is a 'soft option'.

The report discussed the curriculum which should apply to young people in rural areas, highlighting issues such as leaving home, employment and unemployment, leisure, political education, participation and community development, personal relationships, equal opportunities and spiritual development. The authors concluded with the hope that the report would contribute to the debate about the development of rural youth work:

> Action which would enhance the quality of the service's offerings to young people in rural areas and beyond.

The recommendations were:
♦ All organisations and agencies involved in rural youth work should recognise that

enhanced support depends on political and community support at all levels and should take this into account in policies and plans.

♦ Youth workers need:
  • a clear definition of the rules under which they operate and the responsibilities they are expected to bear;
  • aims and objectives which are relevant and easily understood;
  • access to finance, and clear guidance on the budget available to them and the extent of their authority for expenditure;
  • appropriate curricular materials;
  • participation in decision making and regular monitoring of aims and objectives; and
  • training for setting up and managing scattered rural networks.

♦ The role of local authorities should be to collaborate with voluntary organisations in:
  • encouraging development of support networks between statutory and voluntary sectors and between voluntary agencies; and
  • providing and stimulating the preparation of support packs.

♦ Local authorities and voluntary organisations and other agencies should encourage:
  • provision of non-managerial support, where necessary across agency boundaries;
  • peer group support, through networks allowing informal contact, mutual support and learning; and
  • community support, including participation of 'adult' organisations in youth service activities.

As with Thompson before it, the NACYS report became a benchmark, enabling those who had the will to press for change within their own authority or organisations.

Considerable ground remained uncovered, however. Mary Tyler (⁹¹), writing in *Youth in Society* in November 1987, noted that despite all the recent initiatives, rural youth work remained low on the policymakers' list of priorities. She reported on a NYB survey in 1987 which found no existing full and officially-endorsed policy statement on rural youth work in the statutory youth service (as opposed to working group papers and consultation documents). Just one voluntary organisation, the National Federation of Young Farmers' Clubs, had at the time produced such a document. The article provides a useful picture of the then existing range of rural youth work responses and notes particularly the role of peripatetic part-time staff in providing support to workers and improving the quality of youth work in a geographical area.

In 1990 the National Association of Youth and Community Education Officers (NAYCEO) (⁵⁷) issued a policy paper on youth work in rural areas which acknowledged that the needs of rural young people had not attracted sufficient resources from the youth and community service. Using the NACYS report as a guide it set out ways in which members should implement the NACYS recommendations in the areas of curriculum, training and resources.

3C
The Growth of Networks and the Development of Practice

Rural practitioners organising and demanding attention have been central to redressing the historical neglect of youth work in rural areas. By the end of the 1970s/early 1980s the lobbying of the CRY helped to establish the Rural Youth Work Education Project at the then National Association of Youth Clubs. Some good quality publications resulted which helped to make the case more clearly and forcefully. The Rural Impetus Group which followed this project and the subsequent National Rural Youth Work Network have both been influential in lobbying for greater priority to be given to rural youth work issues.

When the NAYC established the Rural Youth Work Education Project in 1979, rural youth work was at its lowest ebb. It was possible for the project director, Michael Akehurst [3], to write in his book *Groundwork: Young People and the Youth Service in the Countryside* (1983) that rural youth work at the start of the RYWE project was:

♦ of low status;

♦ lacked an established body of knowledge;

♦ was under-resourced;

♦ had no distinctive methodology; and

♦ had developed little in the way of support.

His work, however, must be counted as the beginning of the resurgence of interest, spearheaded by rural practitioners. *Groundwork* constituted the first coherent modern statement on attitudes to the countryside, the state of local rural services, the position of young people in rural areas and the nature and status of rural youth work.

The isolation of rural practitioners prompted the publication of *Fieldwork – An Aid to the Support of Youth Workers* [2] in 1984. This handbook sought to enable rural workers to identify and find the kinds of support they needed using illustrative examples.

The NYB made its first substantial contribution to the literature with *Shadows of Adolescence* by Allan Kennedy in 1984 [45] which examined in depth the experience of young people growing up in rural Dorset. Through interviews with young people and his own local knowledge he was able to document the silent withdrawal of young people who had no significant engagement in their local community. As he summarised it:

... in West Dorset many adolescents are powerless to participate in the process of influencing their own futures. As a result they become alienated from the communities in which they live. They are marginal to the rural social

systems operating in the area and from this point of view may be regarded almost as outsiders.

This developing new national focus for rural youth work resulted in the first National Symposium on Rural Youth Work held in Buckinghamshire from 10-12 September 1985, and attended by 84 participants. The report [18] of the event indicates that the major part of the symposium was given over to the discussion of the approaches illustrated by the four case studies presented from Aylesbury Vale, Shropshire, Lancashire and Nottinghamshire, and the identification of issues and problems experienced by rural youth workers.

The list of recommendations from the group includes the establishment of an effective national communication network for all youth workers in rural areas, with the regular publication of information on provision and developments in rural youth work and the organisation of future events.

This need led to the formation of the Rural Impetus Group with the stated aim: 'to raise and maintain an awareness of issues affecting young people and those who engage with them in rural areas of Britain'. Fabes and Knowles [32] provide a list of the nine objectives of this group and note that it is open to part-time and full-time workers, officers, trainers, academics and policy makers in a personal capacity.

The NYB and Lancashire County Council brought together people from the rural youth work field in 1986 at a second rural youth work symposium held at Borwick Hall, Lancashire from 22-24 September [63]. Workshops on action research, curriculum, support and unemployment were held, and examples of practice were presented covering rural housing initiatives, employment in rural areas and specific projects including Chew Valley Youth Work Development Project Research Programme, Brathay Rural Enterprise Project and Hereford and Worcester Youth Service Rural Development Projects.

A survey by NYB in 1987 led to a paper by Catherine Walker [95] summarising the current state of developments in rural youth work. This showed the beginnings of initiatives such as mobiles, the establishment of specialist rural youth work posts and early working party reports on policy and practice.

The third national rural youth work conference was held in Somerset from 30 September – 2 October 1987 [87]. Twelve discussion groups took place, making responses to the four key themes of the rural youth work subcommittee's draft provision paper: the features of rural youth work; curriculum; training; and support.

This was to be the last national event of its kind for four years until the National Rural Youth Work Network, in cooperation with Norfolk County Council Education Department, attempted to hold a two-day event, Encouraging New Partnerships in Rural Areas, in October 1991.

The planned Norfolk event ultimately did not take place due to low take-up but it became possible to hold a one-day event instead on board HMS President moored on the Thames. This proved to be one of the more unusual rural youth work conference locations, and the event, under the title Lessons from Contemporary Practice, examined aspects of both rural policy and practice, highlighting case studies of youth work in rural areas that demonstrated a range of partnerships between statutory and voluntary organisations, the independent sector and commercial sponsors. Four examples were described in detail: the Duke of Edinburgh's Award scheme operating in North Hertfordshire/Cambridgeshire; the Youth Enquiry Service in Skipton, North Yorkshire; the Groundwork project in East Durham; and a mobile project in Shropshire.

Of the regional events that took place between 1988 and 1990 three were well recorded – East Midlands, Lincolnshire and Northern region.

Practitioners in the East Midlands organised an event in April 1989 at Nottingham University [68]. The conference focused on

support networks for youth workers in rural areas. Additionally workshops took place on a wide range of issues including work with travellers, work with girls and young women, health promotion, political education, sexuality, housing, homelessness and leaving home and youth work in depressed mining areas.

The rural youth work conference organised by Lincolnshire County Council Youth Service and Lincolnshire Council for Voluntary Youth Services was held in March 1990 [52].

A northern rural youth work weekend, organised by the Regional Youth and Community Development Unit and held at Beamish Hall in County Durham in September 1990 [72], looked at girls work in rural areas, a mobile project, managing and resourcing rural youth work, using photography as a medium for participation, rural community work and the use of issue-based games.

There are now two parallel national networks of rural youth work practitioners active in England at present. The Rural Impetus Group was established in 1986 and has been a presence in all the major rural youth work initiatives since then. In May 1991 the group reviewed their work and re-affirmed their objectives, which can be found in Ray Fabes and Cherie Knowles' book, *Working with Young People in Rural Areas* [32]. Rural Impetus produces a newsletter which is available on subscription.

Many members of Rural Impetus are also members of the National Rural Youth Work Network which was first convened by NYB in 1987 and has met twice a year since then. It acts as a forum for any manager or practitioner who wishes to share their practice, to discuss issues which affect them and is willing to act in a collaborative way when necessary. The group was formally involved in making responses to the series of ministerial conferences on youth work organised by the NYA. It made a presentation at the Third Ministerial Conference on the Youth Service in 1992 [61] on planning and evaluation.

3D
Commentaries on Youth Work in Rural Areas

The earliest comments on the nature of youth work in rural areas are to be found in the official documents and working party reports already discussed. Other general commentaries on this form of youth work have been a regular, if intermittent, feature of the past decade, when practitioners have looked beyond their own local patch to comment on the general scene.

Michael Akehurst was one of the earliest writers to discuss in a systematic way the needs of young people in rural areas and youth work responses to them. In addition to the reports *Groundwork* [3] and *Fieldwork* [2] which came out of the National Association of Youth Clubs projects, he wrote two papers analysing the position of young people and challenging conventional views of rural life. *Until the Fire and the Rose are One* [6], written in 1980, provides an analysis of rural life which contradicts the popular idyllic image. It discussed how young people in some areas coped with this social environment and looked at initiatives taken by the youth service in rural areas.

Victims of Myth: The Situation of Rural Youth in Britain [4], was co-written with David Marsland in 1981 and highlights the mass of difficulties, deprivations and disadvantages encountered by young people in rural areas, and called for further research and serious attention to their needs.

The theme was reiterated in a *Youth in Society* article published in 1980 [5] *Losers on the Rural Battlefield,* which argued that young people too often lose out in the political battles between opposing factions fighting for their own concerns or financial interests – farmers, landowners, conservationists, the heritage and tourist industries and others.

Ian Johnson writing in *Youth and Policy* in 1986, in an article entitled *Rural Life – A Hope for Young People?* [44], described the way in which services provided for rural areas are frequently justified on criteria derived from urban areas. He called for: 'A recognition that rural youth work is not simply urban work diluted, but requires skills and has special priorities.'

He argued that effective youth work in rural areas needed highly mobile, non-centre based workers with an understanding of rural life. Johnson also made a plea for the provision of youth workers who have an instinctive understanding of rural life, who had grown up in rural communities and whose training had developed the specific skills required for working in such environments.

The field received a considerable boost with the appearance of the special issue of *Youth and Policy* devoted to rural youth work in May 1991. Ray Fabes and Sarah Banks [31] provided an article which reviewed the official documentation, examined the emergence of rural work, described young people's perspectives on deprivation in rural areas and looked at approaches to rural youth work. Much of the material was published in the occasional paper *Working with Young People in Rural Areas* produced by Leicester Polytechnic in September 1991 [32].

Claire Wallace, David Dunkerley and Brian Cheal [96] supplied a valuable piece comparing the economic role of young people in rural and urban households in the Southwest. Young people in rural areas were found to be more likely to leave school and less likely to pursue academic training than urban peers and more likely to expect to leave home and look for a job. They found that the dependence of young people in rural areas upon the family was balanced by the dependence of the family upon them. In some circumstances the young person's labour could be a crucial part of the family business.

Robert MacDonald, in an article entitled *Youth, Class and Locality in Rural England* [53] described research investigating the cultural responses of young people in rural areas to the options facing them after the age of 16, highlighting issues of class consciousness. He concludes:

If policy makers hope to form effective policy for youth and if those working directly with young people wish to provide successful schemes and courses, then we must first understand the local, class cultural worlds that underlie and inform the way in which young people make sense of themselves and their localities and, in turn, that shape the steps they take towards adulthood.

More recently Youth Clubs UK returned to the theme of youth work in rural areas with a round-up by Alan Rogers ([74]) of recent publications and activities in the field, reported in an article in *Youth Clubs* magazine in February 1992.

3E
Reports on Issues and Local Surveys

Much of the literature on rural youth work consists of descriptions of youth work practice, but it is becoming more common for reports to contain analyses of particular issues affecting young people. These often take the form of conference reports or research findings. Six themes occur repeatedly: homelessness, disability, gender, employment, racism and play.

Homelessness

Two reports have recently appeared analysing the issue of homelessness in rural areas and its impact on the community, especially on young people. The RDC report *Homelessness in Rural Areas* ([47]), published in 1992, provided a thorough overview of the subject presenting statistics and case studies. A key issue from the latter includes the pressure on local housing stock as more villages come within the travel-to-work areas of larger towns and cities. Evidence that provision for young single people is generally poor in rural areas and that it is becoming increasingly difficult to provide mainstream accommodation for such groups who do not have some form of special needs

was also underlined.

Centrepoint also produced a report on youth homelessness in rural areas in 1992 entitled *Rural Housing for Youth* ([13]), following a conference of the same title held in June 1992. This came to similar conclusions. Centrepoint identified the fundamental issues being a lack of housing stock, a lack of appropriate housing with support, and the unaffordability factor which priced most rural housing beyond young people's means.

Disability

There appears to be little literature on the issue of disability in rural areas as it affects young people. An initiative by the Community Council of Humberside, however, sponsored a survey report entitled *Welcome All Children* ([40]) published in 1992 on the play and leisure opportunities of children with both physical disabilities and learning difficulties living in rural Humberside. The report presented the results of interviews with children, parents and practitioners and is a rich source of information concerning the needs and experiences of these young people, highlighting problems of access and lack of opportunity.

A similar report from Cumbria ([79]) in 1991 presented the results of a survey of hearing impaired young people. Conclusions here identify a need for early diagnosis and information, more proactive work by the youth service, work to overcome the social isolation of young people, a need for better coordination and cooperation, and increased support for both parents and young people.

The Jigsaw Youth Integration Project ([100]) is a national pilot project funded by the Department for Education (DFE) to explore methods and practices that work towards the integration of young people with disabilities in the mainstream youth and community provision of the Ribble Valley in Lancashire. Their report on progress so far describes making contact with youth workers, initiatives on transport, improving access to centres and work on staff training.

Gender

There has been surprisingly little specialist attention to the needs of girls and young women in rural areas published, though the *Working with Girls* newsletter [93] devoted a special issue to accounts of work with girls in rural areas in 1984 which included some analysis of the issues. The particular needs of lesbians were also identified.

A more recent report from Oxfordshire [51] examined the current youth work provision for girls in predominantly rural areas of the country and found very few girls of 14 or 15 still attending youth clubs. In a survey, 21 per cent of clubs and centres felt they could provide separate accommodation for girls to meet on their own. Interestingly, while half the female part-time youth workers saw a need for special activities for girls and young women the other half did not.

Employment

The RDC [88] sponsored a one-year pilot study on rural youth unemployment in 1985, looking at four different rural labour markets in North Yorkshire, Leicestershire, Norfolk and Gloucestershire. The report describes the structure of local rural youth labour markets, constraints on employers and the way in which young people participate in the local economy. Negative experiences included scarce resources to support economic development, little training for local people lacking opportunities for geographical and occupational mobility, use of informal networks for recruitment that reinforce inequality and a sense that the best jobs were being reserved for incomers. The report's recommendations address transport and personal mobility, access to information and advice, training and education, opportunities for self employment and seasonal and part-time work.

Racism

While being on the agenda for many individual workers for a long time, the issue of racism in rural areas has only recently received detailed attention in formal reports. A Commission for Racial Equality (CRE) report published in 1992 [43] examined the extent and nature of racism in four counties in southwest England and reported on initiatives being taken by the various authorities to combat it. The report recorded a disturbing level of racial prejudice and discrimination directed against members of the Black community and described different forms of racism including direct discrimination, violence and harassment in many areas of life including jobs, access to social services provision, education, careers services, the police and within trade unions.

Play

A report from the National Children's Play and Recreation Unit [59] (1991) describes the Children Today project in Devon, one of three initiatives established by the Unit to highlight the importance of play in the development of children and to explore the best way of providing play opportunities for children in rural areas. The report emphasises the importance of partnership among agencies involved in children's play.

More recently an initiative by the Kid's Club Network is developing pilot projects on after-school provision for primary school age children and work-based clubs in rural areas.

Research on Young People's Needs

A number of recent reports have aimed to investigate the range of needs of young people in specific local rural areas in order to provide a basis for policy development. Two examples illustrate the approaches many such reports take.

a) Involving or even led by young people – the Preesall Knott End research project [103] was undertaken by a group of young people supported by youth workers in 1987–88. It aimed to identify the way the youth service should respond to the needs of young people in this small rural community in Lancashire, and looked at young people's needs, existing facilities and available premises. It concluded that there was an urgent need for provision for the whole community as well as young people. Much of the report was written by the young people themselves and as part of the project they produced a tape-slide programme to record their activities and findings.

b) A service-led study – a report published in August 1993 [9] examined the nature of rural youth work in the Vale Division of Oxfordshire County Council. A survey of individuals and groups in the area confirmed that young people felt isolated and experienced a lack of employ-ment prospects, limited choices and opportunities in their leisure time, continual scrutiny from their local community and got the impression that decisions affecting them were made by people with little understanding of their needs. Recommendations included enabling area youth workers to focus more clearly on their responsibilities to rural areas, facilitating the training of part-time/ voluntary youth workers and enhancing current partnership arrangements.

3F
Descriptions of Practice

The largest category of literature on rural work is concerned with descriptions of local practice – usually highlighting the ways in which problems of isolation, distance and inequality of provision have been overcome. By and large, however, this literature is exclusively descriptive with little real analysis of the implications of the methods used.

The first general description of methods was a compendium of different contributions on the subject produced by the NAYC in 1984 entitled *Delivering Rural Youth Work* [58]. One section looked at the village youth club while another examined ways of reaching young people without a building, through phone-ins, newsletters, mobile youth centres, volunteer contacts and a shuttle leisure bus. The support needs of isolated rural youth workers are identified and suggestions such as club net-working are mentioned together with specialist worker support to existing voluntary provision.

A more recent discussion of youth work methods in rural areas can be found in Peter White's six case studies *Working with Rural Youth* [99] published in 1991 as an earlier part of the NYA's RDC funded-project. This presented a mobile in action in Shropshire, work on an estate in Lancashire, enabling young people to help appoint a youth worker in Cornwall, a youth exchange with the island of St Helena, tackling rural racism in Derbyshire and self-expression through art in Cumbria.

Another collection of projects is presented by Alan Rogers [75] in a *Youth Clubs* article in April 1992, which describes a youth newsletter created by young people in a rural area of Warwickshire, a detached work project which devised a programme for 14 to 18-year-olds without a youth club building and a Girls' and Women's Activity Day in the Derbyshire Dales.

Some of the earliest descriptions of rural youth work from the mid 1970s and early 1980s are to be found in the collection of *Youth in Society* and *Youth Service Scene* articles published by NYB in 1985 under the title of *Rural Youth Work* [94]. Contributions from Sussex, Somerset, East Devon, Buckinghamshire and Surrey are included and subjects as diverse as detached youth work, distance learning youth work courses, supporting village clubs, youth counselling, involving the local community and working with the unemployed are covered.

Youth service developments in rural

Cornwall were described in a 1988 *Youth Service Scene* article by Mary Tyler [92]. Activities included a mobile and a video created by young people in Port Isaac highlighting their frustrations.

An earlier *Youth in Society* article (in 1986) on youth work on Exmoor by Marion Silverlock [86] describes the establishment and development over a five-year period of the Exmoor Youth Association, a grouping of small youth clubs operating across a large rural area which aimed to provide support, liaison and interaction.

A detailed report on work with travellers in Nottinghamshire was produced in 1992 [67], and there are also descriptions of a wide range of youth work practice methods in rural areas in two of the local authority policy documents, *Rural Youth Work in Nottinghamshire* [97] and *County Rural Youth Work* [77] published by Buckinghamshire County Council, and in a report from Lancashire County Council *Identification of Good Practice in Rural Youth Work* (1987) [78].

Two recent reports [84] [85] from the northern and southern areas of Shropshire also contain examples of practice including youth exchanges, work with girls, arts work and personal support to young people in a variety of circumstances.

In 1994, the NYA published a rural youth work training pack [62] which fills a gap in training resources for full-time and part-time youth workers and volunteers working in rural settings. This contains material for a 12-hour training programme covering issues affecting the lives of young people in rural areas, meeting their needs, how to introduce the concept of curriculum, where to find resources for the work and how to raise the profile of youth work within local power structures.

Mobiles

The mobile youth centre has emerged as a major form of youth work response in rural areas in recent years and there is a growing literature on this form of practice.

The directory of rural mobile projects, *Rural Mobiles* [33] published by the NYA in association with De Montfort University in 1993, provides an overview of 46 mobile youth projects currently operating throughout the country. This is the first report from a three-year research project based at De Montfort University which will involve future publications examining features of effective practice.

The National Playbus Association [82] produced a report in 1992, written by Kenneth Shanks, examining the use of mobile units in a range of youth work settings – both urban and rural – through a series of case studies. One of the studies describes the Pegasus project in Northamptonshire which started travelling around the villages in the county in 1989. Some earlier practical advice on going mobile was presented in a book of the same name by the Mobile Projects Association [11] in 1987. A further overview of practice can be found in the *Working with Wheels* report published by the NYA in 1992 [61.1] following the conference of the same name convened in April 1992 as part of the RDC-funded project.

There have also been project reports from a number of different mobiles over the years. Among the most recent are reports from the Sandbach Area Mobile Youth and Community Unit in Cheshire [21] – which was also featured in a *Young People Now* article in 1991 [12], a community youth bus in Kent [69], a mobile in Hampshire [28], a community bus operating in a rural area of Teesdale [19], one of two mobiles operating in Shropshire [29] and the Interlink bus in Northamptonshire [66]. A video produced by Leicestershire Council for Voluntary Youth Services describes the work of three rural youth work projects, two of which are mobiles [50].

3G
Voluntary Sector Youth Work with Young People in Rural Areas

A high proportion of youth work in rural areas is carried out by voluntary bodies, including churches, local representatives of national voluntary youth organisations, such as the Scout Association, Duke of Edinburgh's Award, the Guide Association, St John Ambulance and Young Farmers' Clubs, plus many entirely local projects. As a consequence, most face-to-face contact with young people in rural areas is made by volunteers. Many workers, especially those working outside the established voluntary youth work sector, can find themselves unsupported, with only occasional contact with other workers and often reduced access to beneficial support and training opportunities.

Despite high activity levels, few national voluntary youth organisations have published policy documents on work in rural areas which look at the implications of rurality on the needs of the young people they work with. During the course of the RDC project at the NYA, voluntary sector organisations and projects were regularly requested to lodge documents and reports with us. What follows below is a brief description of the papers and reports that were received, as well as those already in the library collection.

The National Association of Youth Clubs (now Youth Clubs UK) was a clear pioneer in assessing the needs of young people in rural areas and the reports from its Rural Youth Work Education Project in the early 1980s by Michael Akehurst have already been discussed. More recently it has joined forces with the Leaving Home Project and has been involved in a two-year Department for Education-funded programme with youth projects in rural areas, assisting young people to undertake surveys in their local area reporting on the expectations of young people leaving home and the experiences of those who have already left. This is described in their newsletter [49].

Work has also gone on with Youth Clubs UK member projects during 1993 in Gloucestershire, Cornwall and Devon with the Leaving Home Project providing training and consultancy. Youth Clubs UK is also embarking on a three-year project with part funding from the RDC to support workers involved with junior age children in rural settings.

In 1984, a report entitled *Keeping Them Off the Fields?* [16] described the establishment of a Rural Youth Clubs Association in North Lancashire. Voluntary youth leaders in a number of neighbouring clubs were brought together and had the opportunity of organising joint or inter-club events, to swap ideas and share problems at social events. Regular contact was offered by the local full-time rural youth worker, including the setting up of a forum for discussions on youth work philosophy. A *Youth Service Scene* article in 1985 described the practice one year on [81].

Youth Work in the '90s: A Review of Year Three – September 1989 to August 1990 [98] described a collaborative venture between West Yorkshire Youth Association and Humberside Youth Association concentrating on the 16 plus age range. This aimed to broaden the youth work curriculum so that rural youth clubs could become good providers of social education, rather than poor providers of recreation. The project developed a personal development programme for young women, an arts-based basic training programme for part-time workers, a competence-based training programme for workers and an innovative training programme for young people exploring how they could take on roles traditionally occupied by youth workers.

Cambridgeshire Association of Youth Clubs received three years funding from the Gulbenkian Foundation for a rural arts project. Jacqui Hogan [41] described some of the outcomes in an article in *Youth Clubs* magazine and put in a plea for continuity of funding so that achievements were not dissipated through lack of support.

Cumbria Association of Youth Clubs [20] produced a report about itself in 1992 which explicitly identified the importance of its work in rural areas. Key aims for this included:

♦ identifying the distinctive rural youth work method best suited to meet the needs of local young people;

♦ planning ways to establish effective support structures that are vital for isolated youth clubs such as 'club clusters' and district associations;

♦ sharing good practice with others in similar work situations; and

♦ promoting a range of training opportunities for rural youth workers.

The National Federation of Young Farmers' Clubs has long been active in rural areas – since 1921 when the first club was formed at Hemyock in Devon. In a paper making a statement about the Young Farmers' Clubs' role in the 1990s [60] the Federation pledged it would:

♦ stay in tune with rural values;

♦ cater for the personal and social development of young people;

♦ encourage recreational programmes with a learning element;

♦ maintain a strong countryside element in those programmes; and

♦ encourage members to play a full part in the decision-making process of their local communities and the organisation.

From April 1993, the Federation will be using a grant from the DFE to develop initiatives with young people covering issues such as work with girls and health education.

The Scout Association introduced a new initiative called Scoutreach in 1991 to improve contact in areas and settings where young people had not previously benefited from scouting activity. The paper *Scoutreach in Rural Communities* [37] discusses the drawbacks to life in rural areas and recognised the potential isolation of young people living in small communities. It provides advice on finding adult volunteers and securing a meeting place. Importantly it also identifies situations in which normal membership rules can be relaxed to allow for innovative responses to logistical problems. The booklet *Planning and Managing a Scoutreach Project* provides additional practical information [36].

The Duke of Edinburgh's Award planned something similar in 1988 when it set up a new initiative to foster increased take-up of the scheme in rural areas. The discussion paper *The Duke of Edinburgh's Award Scheme in Rural Areas* [25] submitted to the Special Project Committee noted that the objective of the scheme was to ensure that young people in isolated communities and without readily available transport could still participate in the Award. It was intended to seek allies in other rural organisations and use a variety of proven models of delivery such as village networks, part-time field workers, parent-teacher associations, Young Farmers' Clubs, mobile youth clubs and parish council sponsors.

The Duke of Edinburgh's Award rural initiative proposed to build on pilots by funding projects where Award participation had previously been weak. It aimed to act as a pump primer and to tap into existing organisations or networks. A report on those Award schemes was published in 1990 entitled *Special Projects: Inner City and Rural Initiatives* [26]. This reported the results of a pro-forma circulated to projects taking part in the scheme and described developments in England, Wales, Scotland and Northern Ireland.

Although church-based youth work is extensive in rural areas, there appears to be little documentation of this in the form of either policy or practice reports. There are exceptions, however.

The Methodist Church's pack *Young Ideas: A Resource Pack about Rural Churches and the Under Twenty-Fives* (1986) [54] took the form of a series of worksheets designed to help Methodist Church leaders in rural areas think about how to make the most of their existing resources and people, develop local leadership and work with other denominations to promote youth work and draw more young people into the church.

The Methodist Church is planning a special initiative with young Methodists in rural areas in 1994-95 when groups will be formed to enable young people to have their say on issues which are important to them.

The United Reformed Church [46] produced a similar pack in 1987 entitled *Stepping Forward: A Kit to Enable Rural Churches to Take Positive Steps Towards Meeting Young People's Needs* which was designed to help rural churches explore what they and their communities could offer young people.

The Church of England demonstrated its concern for life in rural areas through its 1990 report *Faith in the Countryside* produced by the Archbishops' Commission on Rural Areas [1]. It confirmed that, from a research perspective, the church's work among teenagers is a particularly neglected area of study. The Commissioners put forward a model of how a key person nominated to be a local church's contact with young people could be linked into a support network, but concluded that although there were some examples of good practice the general response of the church to the needs of older young people was poor and more effort was needed. This point was taken up by the Church of England youth service and young people in rural areas were made a target group for pilot programmes of youth work.

Some examples of successful contemporary church youth work are available from Leicestershire and Berkshire. The Churches Outreach Project [71] in Leicestershire was initiated by two local youth and community development workers who were concerned about the apparent lack of contact between young people living in remote south Leicestershire villages and their local parish church. The initiative has involved ecumenical contacts with other Christian groups with support from a local educational charity and the Parochial Church Council. The Parish Youth

Group has enabled isolated young people to meet regularly as a group and activities have included a residential narrowboat project described in the report *Waterway Wanderings* [70].

In Berkshire, a project within the Oxford diocese appointed a rural youth worker to liaise with a group of churches, setting up pilot projects which stimulated new work with young people. A support network for church youth leaders was established which was very well received [35].

Earlier in 1987, The Frontier Youth Trust [73] produced a paper entitled *Rural Frontiers – A Short Study into the Issues Facing Rural Areas and Their Young People Today*. This highlighted the difficulties facing young people in rural areas and encapsulated some of the problems which might be faced by the unwary rural youth worker in the voluntary sector.

3H
Local Authority Policy Statements and Practice Reports

Most of the local authority documentation on rural work originates in the 1980s, when the Thompson Report [90] first put the issue on the agenda at the start of the decade, and the NACYS report [56] confirmed its significance at the end.

In the course of the NYA Youth Work in Rural Areas project, each local authority youth service with a significant rural constituency was contacted in the summer of 1993 with a request for information on the current levels of support for work with young people in rural areas. Documentation and information from 21 authorities (out of a target total of 38) was received in time to accommodate in the text.

Three respondents – Norfolk, Leicestershire and Lancashire – have a longstanding involvement in rural work and have produced reports of practice which identify issues and potential youth work responses or supported rural youth work posts.

Eleven authorities – North Yorkshire ([102]), Shropshire ([83]), Buckinghamshire ([77]), Nottinghamshire ([97]), Devon ([24]), Hertfordshire ([39]), Hampshire ([38]), Humberside ([42]), Derbyshire ([22]), Suffolk ([89]) and Wiltshire ([101]) – have produced a range of documents which function both as policy documents on rural youth work and as guidelines to rural youth workers, although not all have been formally endorsed by local authority committees.

Two authorities – Lincolnshire and Staffordshire – have developed youth work curriculum guidelines which include specialist material on rural work.

Five authorities – Wiltshire, Cumbria, Gloucestershire, Kent and West Sussex – reported that rural work was being supported, including a major new rural youth work initiative in West Sussex.

Practice Reports

Several local reports are worthy of note. A report on local practice in East Hampshire issued in 1984 ([27]) identified the particular needs of its area and made certain recommendations. A subsequent study *Bus Shelters and Benches: A Study of Rural Youth Work in Andover* by Doreen Ashley (1991) ([8]) followed a youth service reorganisation and complimented other policy documents on rural life. Parallel needs were identified and plans for the future set out.

Similarly, Lancashire Youth Service published two detailed documents in 1986 and 1987 which provided a basis for the development of work in their authority. *The Curriculum Development Group Report on Rural Youth Work* ([48]) contained a significant collection of comment and insight on rural work. The group itself was formed after a staff conference with the aim of examining the curriculum used in rural youth work, developing new models of work and

identifying the costs of implementation.

A second report *Identification of Good Practice in Rural Youth Work* ([78]) was a working party report containing ten examples of practice, in many cases illustrating work beyond the conventional range of responses to young people's needs. This formed the focus of their presentation to the third National Rural Youth Work Conference in Taunton in 1987 ([87]).

Policy Documents and Guidelines

It has always been a priority for maintained sector youth workers in rural areas to have their work acknowledged and legitimated by their local authority. In most cases, this has meant creating the opportunity to make statements about the realities of rural work, the needs of young people and in some circumstances to address resource and policy implications. It is notable, however, that documents about rural youth work tend only to appear as additions to existing youth service policies and in only a few cases have rural strategies been fully integrated with existing policies for responding to young people's needs.

The actual process of developing those policies that do exist seems either to be initiated from management as a result of wide-ranging policy considerations, or as a result of grassroots pressure. Both processes can be long – it seems in some cases taking several years before a fully-endorsed policy emerges from the authority.

In some authorities the external stimulus of the Thompson Report ([90]), the NACYS report ([56]) and the ministerial conferences ([63]) have been enough to set in motion internal reviews and working parties designed to reassess authority-wide policy and practice. In some cases, such reviews may have been the first opportunity rural workers have had to express themselves and to ensure that their particular interpretation of youth work was given equal weight alongside other significant issues.

In other cases, the route to greater validation of rural work has been via local practitioner conferences and reports of practice generating responses from management, leading to working parties and policy documents.

Regardless of process, in nearly all instances the existence of rural policies can be traced to the influence of a few key individuals persistently raising the profile of rural work within their own organisation. The 1990s have seen a marked increase in rural youth work policy documents and these are to be welcomed as evidence of a growing commitment to the work. It should be noted, however, that the absence of a policy document should by no means be taken to mean a lack of interest or activity within a particular authority.

The policy documents or guidelines produced so far, although highly variable in length and detail, usually contain three major elements:

♦ a statement of justification for giving special attention to rural areas and rural young people;

♦ a listing of issues affecting young people requiring youth work attention; and

♦ statements on how the youth service can respond to these needs and issues, what the specialised service might look like and how it will enable its staff to work effectively despite the inherent difficulties of the setting.

Some statements draw on a concept of needs or rights pertaining to young people living in rural areas.

Buckinghamshire

Buckinghamshire's policy document [77] asserts the need to redress the balance, arguing for parity of status and resources with urban areas:

> Rural youth work is part of mainstream youth work and will thus be afforded proper status ... The same range of curriculum opportunities will be available to young people in rural areas as in all other parts of the service ... The curriculum will be of the same standard as in other areas of youth work and its content, quality and delivery and outcomes regularly monitored and evaluated.

Devon

> Young people have rights and needs wherever they live, but there is a danger that the needs of (rural) young people are not being given sufficient attention. There is a distinctiveness about life in rural areas, a range of characteristics which call for special responses particularly in view of major social and economic changes now affecting rural communities. [24]

Hertfordshire

> There is a recognised lack of opportunity for young people in rural areas ... The opportunities for personal development including material wealth and career enhancement, are often restricted in comparison with young people in urban areas and so it could be argued that the needs and expectations of young people in rural areas are different. The two aims of rural youth work in Hertfordshire can be stated as:
>
> • to broaden the horizons of young people through as many different experiences and opportunities as possible; and
>
> • to enable young people to fulfil their potential despite the relative inequality inherent in village life when compared to contemporaries living in urban areas. [39]

North Yorkshire

> There are many features which serve to indicate that rural areas for young people are quite different from the picture postcard image many visitors might hold (although) it is unrealistic to depict life in rural areas too pessimistically. [102]

In several instances the concept of rights has been used to emphasise the point that rural areas may be recognised as having a manifest need for additional resources, but they have historically received a less than equal share of the youth service allocation, compared with urban areas.

Issues

There is widespread agreement within current policy documents and guidelines about the range of issues affecting young people that youth work needs to address. Those most commonly cited are: housing and leaving home, personal development and leisure, transport and access, participation and political education, equal opportunities, unemployment, employment, and education and training.

Youth Work Responses

Having stated the rationale for rural work and young people's issues all the documents go on to address how the youth service should respond. There are some variations in the emphasis given to different subjects. Most have statements on delivery issues around premises, equipment and transport, although some are more sketchy than others. Statements on staffing, training and support appear in all documents, but in varying amounts of detail and commitment from the authority. Comments on funding and resource implications only appear in half. Statements discussing partnership are more common, although these are more likely to describe good intentions rather than clear cut policies.

Only the most recent documents reflect the new language of evaluation and performance indicators, which are now a necessary part of the youth work managers' vocabulary. Suffolk's guidelines for example note that:

> *A Development Plan will be produced by the Work with Young People in Rural Areas Management Groups. Contained within the plan will be:*
> *a) strategies for action;*
> *b) targets;*
> *c) performance indicators/outcomes.*

The rural policy documents that now exist provide evidence of the growing understanding of the nature of work with young people in rural areas, but rural workers know only too well the precarious nature of their specialism. As in other sectors of youth work, the possession of a policy giving clear endorsement and commitment cannot guarantee the survival of the work when difficult decisions are being made about priorities between competing sets of needs.

However, clear policies can offer a starting point to further work with young people in rural areas.

4

Youth Work in the 1990s – Responding to Young People's Needs

4A
Clarifying the Role and Purpose of Youth Work

The late 1980s and early 1990s have been characterised by growing clarity about the purpose of youth work and what it achieves in practice. The concepts of curriculum, outcomes and quality have by now entered the language and culture of most youth work in a way that would have seemed unthinkable even three years ago. A number of factors contribute to this including the whole developing culture that requires services at all levels – local authority services and charities alike – to demonstrate their value for money, efficiency and effectiveness.

For youth work, the series of three ministerial conferences that took place in 1989, 1990 and 1992 can be seen as landmarks, bringing together many of the concepts and acting as the catalyst for much recent debate and review. The youth service Statement of Purpose agreed at the 1990 event (64) now offers a basic framework for planning and

delivering youth work based upon four key principles (see pages 1–2).

Although the official status of some of the work of the ministerial conferences remains unclear in that the Statement of Purpose did not receive clear ministerial endorsement, the process prompted many youth service organisations to develop for themselves new policy statements that address the central themes of disadvantage and inequality (see Section 3H, pages 29–32).

For rural work, the youth service Statement of Purpose and the many local interpretations by youth work agencies that build on it give encouragement to imaginative practice. Some of the more developmental work currently taking place is endorsed while the safety of the leisure-based work, which remains the mainstay of much rural club-based work, is challenged.

Much work in rural areas takes place in unpromising settings – in buildings that are often inappropriate, through activities unsupported in both human and financial terms and with little in the way of coordination and training. This means that what is on offer is often ultimately less than what might be regarded as adequate both for and by young people living in other locations. The fact that rural work may often have to struggle for resources should not imply a reduced quality of provision. Indeed many examples exist of the highest quality of work bearing no relation to the formal resources available. In the course of the project we have been inspired by some of the practice we have been able to witness.

The local worker's ability to 'be there' for the young people is fundamental to good practice. The ability to respond positively to young people at times when they seek assistance, to relate to them on open terms, to be emotionally involved, honest and accessible are prerequisites to developing a meaningful relationship and being able to offer a potent socialising influence.

But the question has to be asked – is work that only responds to the here and now needs of young people, or to the agenda set by the adults who happen to be the most influential locally, good enough in the longer term? Will it help prepare young people for the future possibility of leaving behind their roots in order to secure employment, housing or training and to prepare themselves for the increasingly complex demands of maintaining a stake in the rural economy?

Good youth work is concerned with more than simple contact with young people. It builds on positive relationships, provides challenges and broadens the outlook and horizons of all involved. Good programmes have a clear sense of purpose, are coherently planned and have built in ways in which the effectiveness of the work can be measured. Performance indicators, in whatever form they are developed, are relevant and directly aid reflection on what has taken place – helping to plan the next phase.

By this argument effective work with young people is more than the occasional response from concerned adults. The curriculum of rural practice – the substance of what actually takes place – requires accurate engagement with the here and now needs of young people plus a longer term view of those needs as they change. Work with young people in rural areas requires both depth and breadth – tackling a range of

needs and issues at a sufficiently sophisticated level to make a difference to the lives of the young people concerned and adaptable enough to offer progression as the needs evolve.

The starting point for planning any work, therefore, has to be:

♦ accurately assessing the range of needs of the young people concerned;

♦ ensuring clarity about the specific needs and issues that you are going to address; and

♦ anticipating the factors and features that exist locally that are going to make it more or less easy to address those needs – what resources there are in terms of organisations or individuals who are already operating, or are willing to help, set against the problems that are likely to be encountered – resistance, opposition or lack of support.

The sections that follow explore more fully the range of *needs* of young people living in rural areas (4B), some of the difficulties of *delivering a service* (4C), and offer a model of different *styles of intervention* (4D).

4B
Young People's Needs – Looking at the Issues Affecting Young People in Rural Areas

This chapter provides an impressionistic account of the experience of growing up in a rural area, exploring some of the issues itemised later in Chapter 5. It does not attempt to be definitive, but to illustrate some of the themes that make the rural experience so significant for many of the young people that live there.

Isolation

Of the essential features of rural areas, the combination of low population density and distance can create a powerful sense of isolation. There are likely to be few other young people around, and the reality is that you are likely to be a long way away from most public services and amenities.

On a practical level there is the reliance on others to help young people get to where things seem to be happening. Even more important though are the emotional aspects of distance – the potential for loneliness that can be created by feeling far away from where important things seem to take place. Being unable to socialise with others of your own age simply because there are no others, or to be restricted to contact with others who are of the same age but who do not share your perspective on the world, your interests or your values, can be a dispiriting and isolating experience.

There is a distinct risk in not ensuring young people have a breadth of human contact. In some ways the engagement with a wide age range that living in a rural community can confer, means early adult status. But not having the opportunity to experience the unfamiliar, to see or hear a different view of the world can narrow a young person's sense of self.

The regular experience of many young people growing up in rural communities is of being a lone child in an adult world, or the elder sibling with expectations of childcare responsibilities within the family. Adults that a young person does have contact with might be over-protective while pressure on young people to conform to the norms of a small community or of the individual family has the potential to stultify as well as to provide safety and control.

Many reports have commented on the apparent lack of ambition shown by substantial numbers of rural young people, of their apparent passivity and demonstrable lack of initiative. There will be many moments when an observer of young people in rural areas will want to argue that there is nothing passive about the behaviour they are witnessing. But, beneath the bravado or the outward expression of confidence there can often be a more fundamental sense of low self-esteem and

marginalisation that is deeply rooted in the culture of many rural communities and that can create a perhaps surprising sense of claustrophobia.

Visibility

The sense of being far away from where things that matter seem to be taking place is compounded by the way in which those smaller numbers of young people in rural areas are always visible to, and likely to have their whereabouts and behaviour monitored by, disapproving adults.

There is a profound irony in living among the relative open space of the countryside yet without personal space – always subject to scrutiny from others, yet without the potential of the extensive friendship networks and opportunities to mix with other young people usually offered to their urban counterparts. There is also likely to be less opportunity to develop relationships with adults outside the networks of immediate family and parents' friends.

This combination of isolation through distance, dependence on family and friends for their view of the world and enhanced visibility are central themes in the lives of young people growing up in rural areas. Having limited opportunities to mix with others of the same emotional age (emotional because chronological age often belies particular needs) and without the stimulation of meeting others with different lifestyles and cultures, creates a real potential for failing to develop the kinds of social skills necessary to function in the wider community.

Identity

Issues of personal identity are compounded by another set of factors that are often recognisable within rural communities. The parochial, 'small town, backwoods' stereotype is alive and well in many of Britain's rural communities. The cosy rural image perpetuated by those keen to promote country living – from estate agents to lifestyle magazines – ignores those realities. Such images endorse the inbuilt conservatism in traditions and values that can permeate rural life. The reality that power and influence remain in the hands of the few, that decisions remain in the interests of the powerful, that recognisably feudal attitudes prevail and that intolerance can be fierce in its expression, are all features that have the potential to marginalise and oppress young people who express any deviation from the norm.

'Knowing your place' is still a truism in many established rural communities. If you come from the family with a stigma of a generation of 'wrong-uns' your chances of breaking out of the mould are distinctly limited. The same is of course true of the urban youth labelled for his or her family, friends or neighbourhood, but the potency of having the eyes of the community on you at all times is arguably greater within the close – even closed – community that is many rural villages.

Expectations of behaviour can apply in a range of ways. Assumptions and pressures can be exerted over potential career choice – to maintain the family farm, to limit your options to known career routes, to set your sights on the safe choice of job rather than consider something outside the immediate experience of those with the greatest influence.

Even more insidious, however, because they often start earlier, are the sets of gender stereotypes that interplay with factors of class and wealth to present powerful determinants of what is expected of boys and young men and girls and young women. For both sexes pressures to become adult can come early, expectations of helping out in the family business can narrow opportunities for friendship and limit taking part in experiences that extend expectations and give glimpses of other ways of living. If you've got to be up at first light to help with the milking, getting involved in an after-school activity that means you don't get home until late evening can be a

non-starter even if there was transport available. Class and gender stereotypes can combine to provide little tolerance of expectations and aspirations outside the norm – whether simply of dress, outward behaviour or concerning relationships and potential partners.

Parental influence on who your friends are is strong and can be maintained by the simple act of denying transport. The status quo can be maintained at very little effort, making it that much harder for young people to explore friendships and meaningful relationships with those who do not directly receive family approval. Those who step outside what is expected of them can be easily singled out and their behaviour theoretically held in check.

Stereotypes

Extending horizons both in terms of places and people is a valid and important role for youth work. Enabling young people to be informed about the range of future possibilities, being encouraged to fulfil their potential and to explore options that are right for them are features of good youth work in all settings. Encouraging young people to look beyond their immediate experiences is vital. The likelihood is that most rural young people will ultimately have to move away for training, education, housing or employment even if it is their longer term ambition to move back. Issues of racial and sexual identity may well be either outside the experience of adults seeking to influence the destinations of young people living in rural areas or issues they don't wish to deal with. This adds another dimension to the sets of stereotypical expectations that are likely to prevail.

The argument will often go something like 'but there's no race problem here – there aren't any Blacks'. The inherent potential for intolerance present within rural communities has its starting point in many places – strict expectations of young people according to their gender, paternalistic attitudes towards those with disabilities, territoriality, resistance to newcomers, tribalism and, to use a current example, hatred of traveller groups. All of these are rooted in fear of the unknown which can combine to create a powerful intolerance of other cultures and ultimate expression in racism.

Classic assumptions about roles, behaviour and the range of opportunities offered to different groups and individuals highlight the need to engender a positive sense of self in young people. Work with young people in rural areas needs to address all of these at source, tackling difficult issues that are going to be controversial, including those of parochialism and stereotypical expectations – whether by class, because of disability, or by gender or race.

Access Issues

Underpinning the two themes – the isolation of young people and the need to help develop positive identities by tackling damaging stereotypes – is the basic issue of access to the kinds of services and resources that are taken for granted in towns and urban areas.

Little opportunity to become involved with others is one of the most fundamental concerns expressed directly by young people who live in rural areas. Lack of recreational space for young people, for example, can be a surprising problem because of the pressures on land use stemming from former imperatives to press into agricultural use vast acreage of land to maximise output. In some areas access to such leisure facilities will be distinctly seasonal with the added frustration of having to watch holidaying visitors and wealthy incomers enjoying facilities that local young people probably cannot afford in season and have no access to out of season.

Play space for children is often at an even greater premium. The combination of a historically weak play lobby and again a focus on the need for play space in urban areas has meant that the extraordinary position now exists where many rural communities have less land accessible for play than their urban and suburban counterparts.

The village school has always been viewed as an enriching component of rural life. Many village primary schools no longer exist, however. Either they are converted into desirable residences or their empty shells are waiting a decision as to their future The reality is that school for many young people from rural areas means complicated journeys to a settlement large enough to sustain its educational establishment.

The choice of school will largely tend to be determined by considerations of transport. Where parents or carers are able to take this on, options are proportionately increased. Choice otherwise is limited to schools with transport arrangements. For some families the solution is weekly boarding, but this will further distance a young person from other young people living locally and potentially increase their lack of identification with their home environment.

Maintaining in-school friendships out of school are often one of the more rewarding sources of companionship and informal peer support that help adolescents through those years of changing needs. But journeys on the school bus can also mean the enforced company of individuals they least want to be with as well as precious contact time with best friends that they do not get to see enough of.

Working in partnership with the youth service, many schools now play a key role in providing and sustaining high-quality programmes of social education during the day, evenings and at weekends. Many school governors are increasingly keen to develop schools as centres of the community both for young people and adults. Where mutual respect has been developed between schools and the youth service there are endless possibilities for rural secondary schools and those in market towns to be a tremendous source of provision and support for high-quality rural work.

At the point of leaving school and seeking

higher education, further education, vocational training or a job, the problems experienced within school are sharpened. Getting accurate information and guidance about appropriate options is the first hurdle. Actually being able to pursue chosen options is another. Finding an appropriate package of youth training, college or university place could require a great deal of persistence and the support of an effective advocate.

It is at this point that the issue of accommodation and the housing needs of young people becomes apparent. There are increasing pressures on young people of school-leaving age to either begin to contribute financially to home and family or at least to reduce their financial burden on it. Leaving home to undertake a course of study at a far-away academic institution has always been a legitimate means of making the first move away from home in a relatively ordered way with the promise of a support mechanism at the other end. Although ever increasing numbers of young people are taking this route, the proportion of young people from rural areas able to do this is still small.

For the majority, the next move at 16 or 17 is likely to be either to the local further education institute at the nearest town supporting a college, into youth training or directly into a job. The theoretical removal of the 'option' of unemployment following the withdrawal of benefit from most 16 and 17-year-olds in 1988 has particular consequences for young people in rural areas. The jobs on offer are likely to be low on training, poorly paid, seasonal and with either a small employer whose business is being buffeted by the vagaries of the rural economy or with a large employer facing the potential collapse of their market. If the chosen route for a rural school leaver is vocational training, very few local FE colleges and YT schemes are geared up to offer a package of training, accommodation and support. The travel costs to get to an appropriate course may be prohibitive, yet the possibility of securing closer accommodation

may be even more unrealisable.

Faced with either compromising their hopes, sticking with the limited options available locally or trying their luck elsewhere, some young people will take the gamble (with or without parental support) to make the move to the nearest large town. Despite the hope that prospects of jobs, accommodation and training will all be better, the sad reality is that such hopes are often unfulfilled. The phenomenon of young people ending up in bed and breakfast accommodation in declining coastal resorts or in towns and cities is a growing one. It is only relatively recently that research from some of the capital's major providers of crisis accommodation has found the increasing numbers of homeless young people in London originate from rural areas – first via a county town and later the bigger metropolitan areas and cities. Lack of preparation for the realities of securing and keeping accommodation is one of the factors giving rise to homelessness, but the drift to the city because of a fundamental lack of opportunity in the country is the driving force.

There is also the issue of health. Access to emergency facilities is one of the current indicators for degrees of rurality. How long it takes for emergency services to reach a particular rural location is something for all people in rural locations to consider. How long it takes a young person without transport to get to an out-patients appointment at the nearest general hospital is another. The closure of local and cottage hospitals and the centralisation of many resources make it difficult for many people living in rural areas to seek the treatment they need, although it will be interesting to see the effects of the moves towards primary care through Community Health Trust and hospital at-home services.

Getting young people to take health issues seriously is being tackled in many locations by imaginative joint youth service and health education projects which pay careful attention to making the topics important and immediate. However, there are many issues that still need addressing – action on teenage smoking, sexual advice and contraception, first aid, drugs education and more. Acute services and clinics dealing in specialist topics are all going to be located in centres of population while preventative work is likely to reach rural areas last without imaginative commitment to outreach or mobile services.Offering information and advice to young people in a non-labelling way and in confidence is particularly important. Given the reality that in a rural area the prospects of keeping anything vaguely private are reduced – the doctor's receptionist is likely to know the young person's mum, for example – there is an important need for access to trusted individuals who know their way about the system or to actual services that can be approached with the confidence that an individual's anxiety or condition is going to be taken seriously.

Informed choice needs to be the hallmark – accurate information, help to weigh up the options, support to make a difficult decision and practical help without judgment. Independent services (working in partnership with a range of statutory services) have a particular role in that they can cut across organisational boundaries, provide a targeted and non-stigmatising service and be more responsive because of their inherent flexibility and because locally-based staff and managers are more likely to understand local needs.

Anxieties about the incidence of teenage pregnancies or of evidence of risky experimentation with drugs, for example, are often the subject of moral panic in rural areas. The response that uses a combination of education, information and support to those whose activities are causing concern, encouraging them to review their behaviour rather than pressurising young people to 'stop' by public crusade is more effective. Youth services make a particular contribution here with proven experience of making and sustaining contact with young people who are least likely to access traditional services and in the development of harm reduction programmes and peer education projects.

In some rural areas there is increasing evidence of ever younger people gaining access to, and experimenting with, a range of substances. Drugs and substance misuse and the health risks that go with them are not confined to urban ghettos and decaying out-of-town estates, nor should safer sex be the concern of supposedly 'at risk' groups. Informing rural young people about health risks that they are likely to encounter is an imperative, not an option. There is no safety in adopting the belief that 'it' – drugs misuse, prostitution, sexual abuse, domestic violence – is not an issue in rural areas just because the view from the window is more serene.

With all these concerns, the central factor that makes the experience of a rural person different is the ease (or rather the difficulty) of gaining access to appropriate services – for meaningful information, support, treatment or for advice about jobs, employment or education. But physical distance alone is not the only issue. Access to transport is one thing, confidence to use it can be another. Being able to overcome both the practical and psychological barriers to using services away from your own territory all make getting access to many facilities and services a profoundly different experience for young people from rural areas than for others. Add the complexities (or impossibility) of using public transport or the questions that will go with why someone wants a lift and a whole set of barriers come into play that can mean never setting foot out of the door.

This psychological sense of distance, living somewhere where nothing ever seems to happen and where everything you think you want is far away, is a feature that many adults strive for yet young people can find unendingly oppressive. For young people, leaving a town to live in a village can be very detrimental – they leave behind the streetlife and buzz that is such an important part of growing up in towns. Hanging around the village war memorial somehow doesn't have the same sense of 'being there' as meeting your friends at the local nightspot or takeaway.

For young people who have always lived in the country the absence of a legitimate place to hang about and do nothing but be themselves is no less of a loss. Some extraordinary rendezvous points can become significant places for rural young people to congregate, somewhere with a hint of shelter and territory but where you can see what's going on and importantly where you are just about tolerated – near the village chippy, next to the general store, the video shop or out by the water tower on the wasteland that no-one living locally bothers about.

Finding a building that has defensible space and offers territoriality is as important now as it was for earlier generations. Increasing pressure on land use has taken away so much potential 'play' space in rural areas that the irony is it is now easier for urban young people to locate an appropriate empty building – an empty pub or factory unit – than it is to find a rural barn that someone isn't hoping will be snapped up for conversion.

Making do with facilities that would be laughed at by their urban counterparts is one of the realities of growing up in rural Britain. The draughty village hall – available one night a week if you are lucky, and then only as long as you don't disturb the playgroup's store cupboard – is the best that you are going to get in many locations. And no you can't paint the walls because the committee wouldn't like it, the plaque naming the villagers who lost their lives in the Great War cannot be taken down, so there is no chance of indoor sports in case it gets damaged … and by the way, there was some damage to the garden wall of the cottage down the lane three nights ago so we are closing the club until the culprit comes forward.

Escape can become a powerful metaphor for many young people growing up in a rural situation. One vivid manifestation of this is the importance attached to getting your own wheels – witness the number of dubiously roadworthy vehicles and bikes to be seen in many rural settings and the kudos that goes with gaining your own transport and your ticket to independence.

Powerlessness and dependency can be the dominant features for many young people growing up in rural areas. The youth worker's task is to tackle some of these oppressions and to offer experiences that counter the sometimes stereotypical expectations, the lowered sights and the seemingly slow self expression. The reality for youth work is that many of the factors and features that affect young people also get in the way of the organisations and individuals working with them. The section that follows addresses some of these factors.

4C
Factors Affecting the Delivery of Rural Youth Work: Advantages and Barriers

In any given situation there are going to be some factors that are advantageous and others that create barriers to the delivery of an effective set of services to young people. Making comparisons between work with young people in different settings is an obvious but not necessarily helpful activity in that it tends to suggest one or the other is the more difficult or complex. All youth work is demanding. However, there are factors specific to rural situations that require particular skills of the workers that operate there. Solutions for specific rural circumstances need to be tailored to individual locations and the specific needs addressed, but it is also important to learn from the experience of others.

The sections that follow relate to key factors affecting the scope and quality of rural work. Observations concentrate on those features and

factors that seem to occur repeatedly –
appearing in accounts of practice, within policy
documents.

Resourcing

A major factor influencing the extent of current
provision is that throughout its development,
resources for youth work in rural areas have
suffered because there is a compelling if simplistic
argument to concentrate funding where there are
greater numbers of people and where needs
might be more immediately visible. A common
preoccupation in youth work and an often used
indicator of performance is the numbers of young
people being reached. Is the building full? Are
attendances up on the last quarter?

Numbers, however, do not necessarily
equate with need nor does mass with quality.
Although there are likely to be significantly
fewer young people living within a given rural
patch than in other settings, there is an
important counter claim that rural work usually
reaches a higher proportion of young people in a
given area. The absence of the need to cater for
large numbers of young people allows more
time to work directly with individuals, creates
the scope to undertake small group work and,
theoretically, to give greater attention to the
quality of the interventions.

In most areas youth service funding has
evolved piecemeal over many years. This means
substantial anomalies often exist in terms of
levels of funding between similar areas or even
between similar groups. Redistribution along
more equitable lines is a slow and sensitive
process for youth services. Groups already well-
funded whether or nor appropraitely are likely
to be the most protectionist and have the most
political influence to mobilise for retention of
'known' work.

Yet across the whole youth service there are
other losers who are not yet even in the frame,
styles of work and client groups whose needs are
not yet fully met – Black and ethnic minority
young people in urban areas for example, the
need to support specialist work with young

women, action on access to appropriate services
by young people with disabilities, and health
initiatives that reach groups of young people
least likely to access mainstream services to
name a few. Needs as diverse as these have to be
carefully prioritised. Our concern is that the
needs of young people from rural areas do not
continue to be regarded as less valid because
they happen to be taking place a distance from
where decisions are being made.

It is always difficult to secure support for
new work without taking away existing
resources from somewhere else. For some rural
work a combination of two approaches has
been successful:

♦ looking to unlock potential support beyond
   the means of the organisation initially
   promoting the work – seeking funds and
   expertise from a range of local authority
   services, Training and Enterprise Councils
   (TECs), business and commercial sponsors,
   the health authority, the RDC and other
   specialist and local funders; and
♦ delegating decisions about use of resources
   to the local level in order to ensure
   decisions about priorities are made with the
   greatest insights into local needs.

Age Ranges

Work involving young people aged 11 through
to 21 in the same activity at the same time is
not uncommon in rural work. There will be
frequent pressure to extend those age bands in
both directions, to work with younger children
because there is no provision for them and to
work with older young adults because there is
nothing geared to their needs either – the pub
is too expensive or filled with holiday makers
and older local folk, or it is playing the wrong
music and is full of people the young person
wants to avoid.

Devising a curriculum for a village club that
is going to engage this wide age range is far
more complicated than local residents who feel
'something has got to be done' are likely to
appreciate. Young people's needs are not

homogeneous and what might appeal at a given moment to one group may not do so soon afterwards, or at all, to a different peer group. More positively, the spread of ages involved in creating a viable group in many village locations, however, offers the scope to encourage participation – offering progression for young people who might want to take on some specific responsibility through senior member training, for example.

Public Support

Public support is critical to work in rural settings. Not only are young people highly visible, so is the worker. Developing genuine relationships with young people and being their advocate while appeasing the demands of key players in the local community requires a keen sense of humour and a great deal of skill. Demands for containment and diversion are likely to be strong.

An added difficulty is harnessing the goodwill from adults that does exist. One of the acute problems for rural work is to find ways to engage those adults that do come forward – to offer a realistic and rewarding task and to provide support to sustain their initial interest and commitment. Urban youth workers have the prospect of a range of options about the style of work they get involved in, simply because there will be more work going on around them. The same may not be true in a rural setting where many recruits to youth work will be limited in their choice of location and will find themselves expected to be in some way responsible for their charges 'round the clock'.

Declaring a commitment to work with young people in a rural area can be a highly public act within the confines of the local community. This can be too much for some. The turnover of adults involved in youth work is often high, creating constant pressure on recruitment and training. In a rural setting the influence of any one individual who gets involved but then gives up can be such that

serious damage can be done to the prospects of recruiting others and to the cause of the young people that are the target of all the effort. This often results in many local authority-funded youth workers not being local people but travelling in to fulfil their commitment on one or two nights a week.

Inertia

A frequent comment about rural areas is their resistance to change. The cliché that all is static, however, is an unhelpful one. Rural areas are having to contend with massive shifts in the economy, in land use and in patterns of work. Many more (employed) adults are likely to have long travel times to work, for example, balancing a village home life with commitments elsewhere. Lifestyles are changing and tensions between the needs of incomers and long-standing inhabitants can be divisive. The observation that social policy initiatives take longer to gain acceptance in rural areas is not only a function of local reluctance to cooperate but is sustained by widely held desires to preserve the notion of the rural idyll as an antidote to urban living.

The combination of the influence of those for whom change is a threat because it is outside their experience and those who wish to maintain the status quo because they seek the supposed security of rurality conspire to create a sense of denial about some of the realities of rural living. This affects work with young people by serving to underestimate the degree of sophistication needed to respond to young people's needs and the extent of the needs themselves, resulting in a climate of resistance to tackling some of the issues.

The Isolation of Workers

Linked to the variability of local public support is the likely distance from other youth workers operating in similar situations. An important source of support for youth workers are the networks they are able to create with others doing similar work. Enabling workers to exchange experiences, to reflect on their interventions, to express their frustrations or share their successes is an important and legitimate activity that sustains individuals through the sometimes dubious rewards of work with young people and acts as an informal training forum.

Physically meeting other workers on a regular basis to overcome some of the inherent isolation of work in a rural area is logistically difficult and hard to sustain both in terms of time and cost. Finding allies among others operating locally becomes all the more important when the headquarters organisation is at a distance and the line management process far away or scarcely identifiable. Local health professionals, teachers, social workers, police officers and others can all become important allies.

Relationships with Urban Work

The fact that most youth work has its origins in seeking to tackle urban ills becomes significant here. Without a historically legitimate body of knowledge about the needs of rural young people and appropriate responses, rural workers can find themselves cast adrift. Within most organisational settings, both in the maintained sector and within voluntary organisations, the emphasis of the work is going to be elsewhere. Colleagues might find it hard to believe the assertion that there are difficulties about delivering a service in a rural area. Sadly, professional rivalry about who has the most demanding job is an almost inevitable by-product of work within a service that is itself undervalued and to which the public is largely ambivalent.

Ways to find validation for the practice of individual rural workers lead back to the need to create it locally. Given the reality that most direct work will be undertaken by volunteers and sessional workers, there is an added problem of creating the space to provide the degree of support that is necessary. People's

motivation for working with young people is precisely that – to work among them, to see them as individuals with struggles of their own and to share a part of their lives. Creating an expectation of further commitment to undergo training and to take part in supervision is likely to feel at first like an unhelpful diversion from the real task. If such underpinning is absent, however, the need for it is likely to be identified too late with the result that goodwill is lost, effectiveness reduced and disillusionment follows.

Support Needs

Newcomers to youth work need examples of good practice to improve and encourage them. In a rural setting, meeting young people and indeed finding and locating the resources to meet their needs is particularly difficult with premises few and far between and little administrative help. A lack of other models of good practice compounds the situation and, like their urban counterparts, the rural youth worker is all too often left dependent on the development of relationships with young people with few back-up resources.

The Manager's View

From the perspective of a service manager in either the maintained or the voluntary sector, the problem is reversed. The isolation of individual workers, the reliance on volunteers and the reality that supervision can only take place at a distance means that there may be occasions where a manager has difficulty keeping abreast with what is going on in the organisation and the service. This can result in inconsistencies in service delivery because of the reliance on the personal motivation, competence and integrity of staff.

To combat this there have been important moves in many authorities including appointing area or patch staff with responsibilities that enhance the oversight of unit workers. This can bring decisions much closer to the ground and ensure greater consistency in service delivery, at the same time as bringing a sharper edge to development and to accountability.

Risks

In all youth work it is necessary to provide a framework for professional delivery including training and support that will nurture offers of assistance from within the local community while safeguarding the needs and interests of young people and protecting them from exploitation. Such a framework is particularly important in order to ensure that the work of individuals or organisations setting themselves up as youth workers is properly and professionally informed and that it is understood locally.

The degree of autonomy many rural workers currently enjoy can of course allow innovation, charisma and imagination to shine through and much effective work has often been in spite of, rather than because of, the setting and the circumstances.

Because rural areas are far from homogeneous, urban eyes will frequently miss the regional variations, the differences in identity between those who live close to market towns and those living in deeper rurality, the range of economic stability and the potency of distance. Styles of work appropriate in one village location may be wholly inappropriate in another setting relatively close by. The section that follows explores some of this variety and develops a model of possible youth work interventions that moves beyond many of the current traditions of rural work.

4D
Developing Models of Intervention

There are many documented examples of someone new to rural youth work being given the seemingly straightforward brief to work among groups of young people in a rural area, to make contact, to find out their needs and to begin to 'do something' about their visible boredom. For the worker involved, this can easily lead to frustration and rapid de-skilling as the needs of the young people they get to know become more complex and real. If an adult worker develops the trust and confidence of young people, it soon becomes apparent that the initially expressed needs for a place to meet and space for legitimate social interaction with peers, are but the first in a whole set of needs that are every bit as significant as those of their urban counterparts yet are more difficult to respond to.

Needs and Responses

The rural worker will not have access to the kinds of specialist resources and support services that are likely to exist in centres of population. Who should they refer to for advice, for instance, when the first group of young people seek hard information and advice about sexual identity or employment rights? Successful rural workers have to develop an extensive knowledge base, all-round competence plus the confidence to deal with whatever comes their way. Meanwhile many within the wider community will have been developing different expectations. They may be hoping for speedy resolution to the visibility issue yet at the same time may want to deny the existence of some of the deeper problems. The public agenda becomes to suppress, to control and to keep out of sight.

The first balancing act for rural workers is to attempt to meet the wide range of young people's needs that they are likely to encounter while still keeping the local community 'on their side'. The second is to create high quality provision that attracts young people, maintains their interests and offers a meaningful and progressive curriculum. The third is to satisfy the funders. Securing funders requires an ever more sophisticated approach. Arguing that needs are getting more complex is far from enough to secure the appropriate resources to tackle them. Workers at all levels are having to demonstrate clear outcomes to their work as funders become more demanding in their expectations of accountability and face more difficult choices concerning priority of needs.

Accountability

Much of the work that takes place in many youth work settings is not going to survive by act of faith. There is not enough credibility to youth work, nor visibility at present, to protect it from the rigours of performance review now expected in all sectors.

Elected members, charitable trusts, commercial sponsors and local government officers are all under increasing pressure to account for their policies and decisions in a way that was unthinkable just a few years ago. There is no immunity from this kind of change. The argument that youth work is primarily about process is no longer enough to secure resources without complementary evidence of the basic need for the work undertaken, in efficiency and its demonstrable benefits in terms of learning or influence on young people's skills, knowledge and attitudes.

Effectiveness

Several studies by HMI (now OFSTED), including the 1987 document *Education Observed 6: Effective Youth Work* and the 1993 report *Effective Youth Work in Clubs and Projects*, give pointers to the key features of good youth work practice. These can be summarised as:

- work having clear objectives based on a common understanding of the values and ethos of the organisation involved;
- skilled individual workers, who have local knowledge and are prepared to intervene in incidents and help people to learn from difficult situations;
- work that is consciously planned, that builds on analysis and reflection of previous work;

- attractive programmes that engage with the needs and interests of young people and that take place in locations that inspire a sense of being valued;
- staffing levels, administrative support and supervision arrangements that enable workers to concentrate on their task; and
- methods of work that genuinely involve young people, encourage decision making, promote action and encourage leadership.

Having a clear sense of purpose for the work and an explicit agenda for work undertaken has benefits on several levels. It makes it more likely that young people are going to get involved in the first place, enables them to get more out of their involvement and gives validation to the worker's task – enabling workers to reflect on what they set out to do and be able to say at the end 'we did it and we did it well'.

Reactive Work and Intuition

Because so much work in rural areas has taken place at a distance from the voluntary organisation's field officer or the local authority's area worker, there might develop a high level of autonomy among individual workers. This can mean heavy reliance on the intuitive skills of the individuals involved. At worst their brief will be vague, the absence of sophisticated resources embarrassing and workers will regret the reduced contact with their line managers. In this kind of scenario, workers can do little more than react to the circumstances as best they can, to make the most of the resources that are available to them and if they are able to plan ahead with any confidence at all, to be able to look little further than 'what shall we do next week?'.

This reactive state is not an uncommon one. In the short term it is genuine and worthy but over time it neither makes best use of the worker's energies nor provides the young people with more than a concerned adult with whom to share their frustrations.

Youth workers often try to tackle too many issues at the same time – seeking to plug the gaps between services and sectors and trying to operate at a range of levels all at once. Work on the smaller scale that the rural setting provides offers an opportunity for focusing practice more clearly, capitalising on the worker's ability to get alongside young people, to understand their needs and to be accurate in their responses. To do this well requires a more strategic approach than is universally evident at present, requiring workers to be clear about the purpose of their interventions and explicit about their hopes for change.

Developing a Sense of Purpose

Clarity of purpose involves clear objectives for young people's learning, increasing participation and anticipating long-term effects on the young people. (See ministerial conference Statement of Purpose [64].)

This more purposeful approach may lead to expected outcomes to the work that have very different timescales – influences experienced now may well only be applied years later. But that is the potency of youth work, to help develop the confidence that enables young people to tackle issues way into the future, long after they are outside the influence of school or parents and – particularly important for rural young people – in preparation for a life that will take many away from their current situation.

Doing this well rests on a number of factors:

♦ ensuring that what is on offer engages accurately with the needs of the young people on whom the work is being targeted;

♦ using a range of techniques to gain attention, interest and trust; and

♦ looking beyond the immediate resources of the individual worker and their organisation to develop ideas and provision.

Allies are sought beyond the initial sponsoring organisation, a range of offers of help identified and a spirit of collective responsibility nurtured.

Objectives are explicit, clearly understood by a range of people and no longer the private agenda of the individuals involved. Other organisations are brought into the picture who may need to be convinced of the validity of a youth work approach and for whom some of the needs and responses will have to be spelt out. At its most effective, work at this level draws on the skills and resources of a whole range of organisations and individuals. Support is secured at the highest managerial level for work undertaken closest to the ground. Joint strategic planning takes place with conscious decisions being made about priorities based on accurate research. Support and training involves a range of sectors with attention paid to the development of meaningful links at a range of levels – practitioner, manager, strategist and funder. Workers on the ground know who they can relate to and where they can seek, and expect to find, understanding and appreciation for what they are trying to do.

This can be described as proactive work – work with a long-term view of the needs and issues that aims to be both effective immediately while planning clearly for future needs by supporting developmental work.

The model that follows illustrates the distinctions between *reactive* work and *proactive* work by highlighting aspects of youth work practice that are, for example, more planned (proactive) or more immediate and intuitive (reactive), are based on a repertoire of changing activities that offer progression (proactive) or a repetitive diet of the familiar (reactive). It does so by linking themes under six headings: entitlement; policies; planning; partnership; support; and curriculum.

The model is of a continuum – there are no absolutes of 'good' or 'bad' for each element. However, work that when measured against this checklist consistently finds itself in the reactive phase is in need of review. Does it engage accurately enough with the needs it purports to meet? Is what is on offer sufficiently stimulating? Can it demonstrate that is makes a significant contribution to young people's lives?

Chapter 5 offers checklists of the range of factors affecting young people in rural areas and appropriate youth work responses to those needs. It gives examples of practice that aim to be proactive. The conclusions in Chapter 7 build on the framework of the six themes used here and suggest specific recommendations.

A Developmental Continuum for Work with Young People in Rural Areas

Reactive Work (Work that is unplanned and largely intuitive)	**Proactive Work** (Work with clear aims and a long-term view)
1 ENTITLEMENT	
Little acknowledgment of the extent of young people's needs	Rural needs explicitly understood and acted upon
Lack of planning	Planned, relevant, challenging, accessible provision offering progression
Repetitive provision	Distinctive practice engaging with changing needs and circumstances
Marginalised work not a priority for other people	Work well coordinated and properly resourced
Little attention to issues of discrimination	Work undertaken within a clear anti-discriminatory framework
Little acknowledgment of the barriers that inhibit some young people's take up	Equality of opportunity made real by close attention to provision
2 POLICIES	
Vague brief given to workers	Clear agenda-setting – work explicit and understood by managers
Little relevant or documented policy	Clear correlation of practice with policy statements
Little likelihood of organisational backing if things go wrong	Explicit (and helpful) policies guide workers
Little or no inter-agency commitment	Explicit support for the work from a range of agencies and individuals
No development strategy	Clear policies with long-term and short-term objectives
Static, narrow policies	Policies determined (and modified) by a clear process involving a range of organisations and interests
Policies for youth work stand alone	Clear reference to young people's issues in other organisations' policy statements

Reactive Work	Proactive Work
(Work that is unplanned and largely intuitive)	(Work with clear aims and a long-term view)

3 PLANNING

Work is in response to what young people say they want	Research identifies hidden needs that work is explicitly planned to address
Work is intuitive, based on workers ideas about what is needed	Needs are consciously researched and priorities consciously determined
Resources are allocated by historical precedent	Resources are allocated according to a clear set of priorities and an explicit means of calculation
Little community support	Community support is nurtured (but unlikely to be unanimous)
Work is based on precedent	Work is evaluated, practices reviewed, effectiveness demonstrated, learning applied
Little or no application of theory is evident	High correlation exists between theory and practice
Little or no managerial awareness of practice	Clear two-way accountability exists between managers, planners and strategists

4 PARTNERSHIPS

The work relies on a single source of funding	Multiple funding creates a buffer to financial stresses
No money available for new work	Development budgets ensure scope for innovation
	Resources of other organisations available
Workers from different organisations meet only at the operational level	Partnerships cemented at executive level and meaningful at all organisational levels
Aims and values of organisation do not seem to be shared by others	Values explored and codified by a mutually agreed statement of purpose shared by all organisations operating locally
Workers seem not to know what other organisations are doing	All local workers are aware of and share in developments elsewhere
Competition for scarce resources evident	Funding bids are approached collaboratively
Work and projects are under resourced and too small to have real impact	Work resourced to a level that ensures effectiveness ('critical mass' theory)

Nothing Ever Happens Around Here

Reactive Work	Proactive Work
(Work that is unplanned and largely intuitive)	(Work with clear aims and a long-term view)

5 SUPPORT

Reactive Work	Proactive Work
The worker feels isolated	Explicit arrangements exist for support and for cultivating a team identity
Over-reliance placed on the goodwill of local volunteers	Clear arrangements exist for the recruitment and support of volunteers valued for what they do
Little training available	Systematic training made available at all levels (for workers and managers) on issues and skills
Little attention paid to the relevance and accessibility of available training	Training, while mandatory, acknowledges individual needs and skills and is appropriate in content, style and timing, organisation
Little support available to harness local goodwill or to tackle resistance from within the local community	Explicit support available from managers and peers to raise the profile of the work or to assist in responding to incidents
Little awareness of the need for supervision and appraisal	Supervision regular, structured and beneficial
Little administrative support available and resistance to imposed systems evident	Administrative needs understood, appropriate administrative support available locally

6 CURRICULUM

Reactive Work	Proactive Work
What is on offer is in response to simple demands from young people	Needs researched – responses relevant to needs
Here and now priorities prevail	Work part of planned curriculum activities
All work is spontaneous	Curriculum planning creates a focus to the work, but leaves space for immediacy
The workers' interests prevail	Range of skills, ideas, approaches and experiences harnessed
Limited repertoire of activities	Fresh activities constantly being sought and introduced – progression encouraged
Little use of materials for discussion	High usage of curriculum materials – some 'off the shelf', others created or adapted locally
Little reflection evident	Clear processes in place for evaluation and the application of learning
Little participation evident	Participation encouraged both structurally and personally and can be evidenced in practice

5

A Framework of Needs and Responses

The following three sections summarise the major factors affecting young people in rural areas, as introduced in Section 4B (pages 34–40). The factors we identify are grouped together under three headings: **isolation**; **identity**; and **access**. Greater detail concerning the impact of particular kinds of rural disadvantage and lack of access to services on individuals' life chances, attitudes, behaviour and well being is given. Checklists of youth work responses illustrating suggestions of the type of action most likely to overcome each of the disadvantages are identified. These are then illustrated by examples of practice which are intended to encapsulate work with a proactive approach – illustrating qualities of innovation, relevance and effectiveness. While we do not identify particular projects, they are nevertheless real examples of work taking place in all corners of the country and from all sectors – the established voluntary sectors, the independent sector, local authority work and within multi-agency projects.

There are difficulties in putting many of these ideas into practice. It has taken a long time for youth work with young people in rural areas to be recognised as a valid area of activity. The blocks to effective youth work delivery are many and varied, including the conservative nature of rural areas, staffing and finance. Nevertheless, it is worthwhile at this stage to identify best practice in order to provide a more equitable and fulfilling lifestyle for young people who are, in many cases, trapped in circumstances over which they have no control.

5A
Isolation

The issues for young people living in rural areas listed in this section are the fundamental ones which arise from being few in number and living in a setting which in numerous cases has been progressively robbed of its capacity to exist as a self-sufficient social and economic unit. This is not to suggest that rural areas are automatically deficient in opportunities for the social education of young people growing up in them, but that such opportunities no longer occur naturally as they may have done when the rural population was larger with greater numbers of young people living there.

Young people in rural areas today will not necessarily experience all the difficulties described simultaneously, but each factor has possible consequences depending on the combination of individual circumstances. Youth workers must assess how far the factors apply to the young people they know and work with.

SOCIAL ISOLATION

The Issues

The small numbers of young people in many rural settings can mean having very few friends. This can lead to personal and social isolation expressed through:

♦ inability to relate to others outside own community;

♦ lack of experience in a range of unfamiliar social settings;

♦ low educational expectations;

♦ sense of marginalisation;

♦ dependence on relationships with adults and little choice;

♦ few opportunities for young people to be their age;

♦ reliance on relationships with siblings (greater isolation still if a lone child);

♦ difficulty in finding others who have similar interests, tastes, ambitions;

♦ parental expectations of help in the home or the family business (including help at anti-social hours); and

♦ little choice of sexual partners.

Youth Work Responses

Youth workers can combat the isolation experienced by many rural young people by creating safe opportunities for them to increase their contact with others – both in terms of

frequency and breadth. Contact with young people and with other adults may be important in order to broaden the range of role models experienced. At its most basic, this means:

♦ creating opportunities for young people to meet other young people in social settings – activities, trips and events;

♦ introducing individual young people to others in similar situations;

♦ encouraging contacts between peers (by helping create networks and mutual support); and

♦ getting to know a rural patch, its people and its needs.

Key tasks for the youth worker are making contact and developing meaningful relationships with young people and recruiting and supporting adults who can offer some positive involvement in young people's lives. Initiatives can include:

♦ recruiting local adults to help with skills sharing, hobbies and leisure interests – such volunteers may not need the full range of youth work skills, but can compensate by their availability;

♦ making contact with young people at their chosen meeting places – for example, next to the telephone box – and enabling them to articulate their needs; and

♦ organising activities or transport to facilities elsewhere – this might include complex rendezvous arrangements, seeking parental approval and taking careful note of the territoriality of peer groups.

Practice Examples

♦ There are particular problems in organising Guide units in sparsely populated areas. In a large rural northern county, units are set up in villages by adult leaders who are supported by a network of advisers and trainers who travel large distances throughout the county. The Guide Association sets up self-help systems to assist with transport to overcome communication problems. A system called lone guiding helps girls living in extremely isolated circumstances. Girls communicate with a lone Guider by telephone and letter and can in this way be members of the Association even though they cannot attend unit meetings. A mobile Ranger unit (for girls aged 14 and over) helps to link girls from different population centres who meet in different areas each month.

♦ A three-year project was established in East Anglia as a partnership between the RDC, the local authority Community Education Service and a local voluntary youth organisation. The project seeks to recruit as part-time workers adults who are themselves living in isolated rural communities to target young people aged 14 and over who are not attached to any existing youth work provision. The purpose is to provide:

♦ new self-help groups and projects in rural areas;

♦ issue-based projects;

♦ participation schemes; and

♦ collaborative links with other agencies.

The first year of operation demonstrated a need for activity-based one-off programmes, counselling/information services and cheap transport in rural areas.

♦ Part-time workers in a southern county use detached work methods to make contact with young people in villages which have no youth work provision at all. Five different places are covered on a regular basis with staff available between 7.00pm and 10.00pm. The young people contacted are in the age range 14 to 25, although most are between 19 and 22 and mainly male. Staff befriend young people and offer an information and referral service in response to queries that come up. Specific support can be offered to young unemployed people – for instance, putting together, typing and printing a curriculum vitae on a lap top computer. Information on occupations/careers advice and training is available. Transport can be offered from particular villages.

♦ An area worker organises a peer telephone network, used to organise rendezvous for transport, to plan activities or just to keep in touch with each other. The worker offers a place to meet, a range of activities and access into wider activities via the County Association of Youth Clubs and the LEA.

♦ A Crusader group in a very isolated fenland area provided the only youth work contact for 10 young people aged 8 to 14. The group met mid-weekly in the home of an adult member with three other leaders and provided a place to meet, gave them the chance to develop relationships and organise activities.

LONELINESS

The Issues

Young people in isolated communities have few opportunities to relate to other young people with similar interests or needs. But friendships are a vital support during childhood and adolescence and the medium through which young people share most of the ups and downs of growing up. Enforced loneliness can lead to:

♦ inability to share feelings and experiences both as they happen and in later life;

♦ limited skills in relating to other young people of the same or opposite sex;

♦ narrow personal relationships now and in the future;

♦ limited options for future life partners;

♦ high levels of personal anxiety and potential for later depression, mental health problems;

♦ over-anxiety about emerging sexual identity during adolescence;

♦ little interest in the outside world and boredom; and

♦ lack of drive and low self-esteem.

Youth Work Responses

Youth workers can offer an important and non-stigmatising support mechanism for rural young people who express some of the more profound manifestations of loneliness:

- using interpersonal skills to assist young people to express their individual hopes and fears;
- creating 'safe space' for young people;
- putting young people in similar circumstances in touch with one another;
- introducing young people to examples of problems and services elsewhere that legitimise their concerns; and
- sensitively targeting their efforts on young people observed to be particularly withdrawn.

By working at a more strategic level, youth workers can also sensitise other services to respond more effectively to the needs they observe – working with other organisations to introduce new facilities or to make existing provision more accessible, relevant or responsive. They can:

- stimulate and coordinate a network of existing provision for young people in an area to maximise its potential and focus its response to needs;
- organise events that introduce local young people to the work of a wide range of agencies – health, housing, advice agencies;
- bring together local providers to explore the needs of young people in a particular location and to coordinate responses – health education, GPs, careers, probation, social services, schools, TECs, mental health projects;
- work with the commercial sector and local councils to make leisure facilities more accessible; and
- sensitise local adults to young people's needs.

Practice Examples

♦ A youth project on the Welsh Borders provides information, advice and support to young people aged 16 to 25 who have left school and therefore no longer have a ready-made support network available to them.

An advice line is publicised and workers are also prepared to travel to meet people face to face.

While some enquiries are self-referrals, other contacts are received through social services, nurses, local clergy and mental health services. Five youth advisers each work four sessions a week and follow up enquiries with responses which may range from immediate information and advice, to four or five face-to-face contacts or long-term support. Issues covered include housing, employment, transport, social activities, loneliness, shyness, relationships, benefits and health.

The staff do not offer long-term counselling, but offer support to individuals to help them seek for themselves the help they need. For example, workers were able to help young people who had had treatment for mental illness reintegrate into their local community, helping them overcome the extreme loneliness and isolation that was at the root of the problem.

♦ A youth programme on a local BBC radio station goes out on a Friday evening between 7.00pm and 9.00pm. It acts as a lifeline for young people in the surrounding area who might otherwise feel cut off from youth activities. Twelve young people aged 16 and 17 volunteer their services as reporters and presenters and decide on the content of each programme, researching the items and learning the skills of studio editing as they go. Some are at school or colleges, others are working or unemployed.

The station received a grant from the county council which is matched by the radio station. The programme aims to cover issues of importance to young people in an attractive way, interspersed with information on games, music, cinema and local youth club events. Young people tend to be involved for two or three years on average. Many are able to get jobs on other radio stations, having learnt the basic skills, or apply their experience in other jobs.

♦ A part-time worker with the brief to work within a school catchment area first makes contact with young people on the school bus, offering initial befriending, then access to activities and social space for a number of young people in similar circumstances.

LIMITED MOBILITY

The Issues

Lack of access as a young person to the personal transport that many adults take for granted is a fundamental issue for rural young people. Specific difficulties are created that:

♦ make it impossible for young people to do anything or go anywhere without (complicated) advanced planning;

♦ mean others always know where young people are going, who they are with and what they are doing;

♦ make it difficult to develop or maintain contact with friends;

♦ severely restrict times when it is possible to get involved in activities elsewhere because of reliance on parents (or friends) to provide transport; and

♦ introduce a risk factor unacceptable in other circumstances – hitching lifts, walking late at night on unlit roads or using unsafe or illegal vehicles.

Youth Work Responses

Appropriate responses include:

♦ recruiting volunteer drivers willing to use their own cars to transport groups of young people to events;

♦ organising self-sustaining networks of parents willing to provide transport on a rota basis;

♦ providing access to minibuses via local pools with attention to driver training, maintenance, insurance arrangements, safe parking and location in order to reduce long round trips;

♦ pre-driver training programmes – especially off-road initial skills training for moped users, motorcyclists, potential car drivers;

♦ loan schemes for basic transport – using mopeds, commuter bikes;

♦ lift listings, transport networks, telephone timetables;

♦ coordination of regular (non-commercial) minibus routes into local youth provision;

♦ influencing commercial (and other) providers to introduce new routes and modify timetables to improve access and return journeys to urban provision; and

♦ use of Royal Mail post buses, investigating scope for subsidies, price packages on certain routes, times to coincide with access to leisure facilities in nearby towns (district council involvement).

Practice Examples

♦ Youth workers at an urban youth centre in the East Midlands noted an increase in young people using the nearby sports facilities. Young people from outlying rural areas had discovered a bus which could get them into town and out again at convenient times, but staff at the sports centre were unable (or unwilling) to work with the increased numbers of users. Tensions were leading to conflict and incidents of property damage were being attributed to this group.

The urban youth workers began to get involved, diverting some of the tensions and negotiating a better deal for the new rural users. This led to increased access to a wider range of facilities at the centre on the basis of supervision being provided by the local youth work team.

After a time the youth workers were able to negotiate with the bus operator for a single ticket that included both the bus fare and access to the sports centre at a fixed price. Rural young people living further away ceased to be doubly disadvantaged by the distance and gained access to sophisticated provision that met many of their leisure needs and enabled them to mix with existing friends and meet new ones in a safe and disciplined social environment. They were also able to learn something about how to influence provision – getting adults to listen to their needs and to take action to respond.

♦ Many rural youth projects use a variety of methods to ensure young people in outlying areas are reached and enabled to take part in activities. Mobile projects, in particular, are used in a variety of ways to help transport young people to activities or to bring activities to them.

A youth club in a rural fenland district offers a guaranteed get-you-home scheme to attenders from outlying villages. Staff give young people lifts home at the end of the evening with built-in safeguards to avoid one-to-one situations. Young people pay a charge which is then used to reimburse staff for petrol costs.

♦ A group of local workers and volunteers network their clubs by 'twinning' arrangements – sharing resources and offering transport from one location to another to offer a broader range of activities more evenings per week. Friendships grow and young people in different settlements gain access to other young people and experiences outside the immediate local community.

♦ A youth service in the Southwest has looked at ways of collaborating with other agencies to organise dual use of their minibuses at times when they are not needed for their main purpose. A school meals service, based in a rural area, used vehicles to deliver meals during the day between 11.00am and 2.30pm, but they were not in use during evenings and weekends. The youth service arranged for the four vehicles to be equipped in such a way that they could be used either as vans or minibuses and negotiated access to them at evenings or weekends when they could be hired by rural youth groups. The meals service kept responsibility for maintenance and the youth service handled the allocation of vehicles to groups.

In a similar way they negotiated dual use of minibuses owned by a local college and a student union which were not being used during summer holidays.

NARROW HORIZONS

The Issues

To some people living in isolated communities, the next valley could be on a different planet. Balancing local identity and traditions with knowledge and understanding of what is going on elsewhere is essential to growing up in multicultural Britain. A narrow perspective held as a young person can lead to:

♦ labelling according to social expectations of family/local community;

♦ non-take up of later opportunities for education or training due to limitations of tradition;

♦ fear of mobility – staying put regardless of job prospects;

♦ putting up with reduced life chances;

♦ pressure to conform, stay put and fit in; and

♦ difficulty in rehearsing to be adult through limited role models and the impracticality of exploring other life styles.

Many rural young people's lack of familiarity with urban experience can make for unrealistic expectations of it and may lead to:

♦ inability to access provision in urban settings due to lack of confidences; and

♦ negative assumptions about people from other areas concerning their attitudes, values or behaviour – at its most innocent level this can lead to misunderstandings, but more seriously to intolerance, disputes over territory and to racism.

Youth Work Responses

Youth work can make an important contribution to broadening horizons by:

♦ offering insights into life elsewhere – life in a larger town perhaps – or life in an urban environment;

♦ offering international comparisons of rural living;

♦ asserting a sense of place – encouraging

understanding about where young people currently live, its geographical features and resources and its relationships with other places by trade, migration;

♦ organising residential exchanges with groups of young people elsewhere – village to village, village to urban setting, village to other European village;

♦ simple networking with groups of young people from elsewhere for activities and social events; and

♦ identifying the significance of territoriality, tribalism and its potential for tension and disharmony tackled through active group work and the use of curriculum materials.

Practice Examples

♦ Youth workers in the West Midlands organised an exchange in which a group of 24 Danish young people and 4 Danish youth workers visited the county. Various visits to schools and clubs were organised enabling groups of English and Danish young people to share experiences and remove the barriers and stereotypical views of each other's countries which existed before the exchange. The English group started fundraising for an exchange visit the following summer.

♦ A group of young people from village youth clubs in the Home Counties visited the European Parliament in Strasbourg and joined together with over four hundred young people from all over the European community to debate issues that were important to them. A visit to Paris was included on the way home. Many of the young people involved had never been out of the country before.

♦ A group of young people from a small market town in Devon visited the Notting Hill Carnival in London for three days as hosts of one of the steel bands appearing in the carnival. A return visit was organised for the band to Devon and both experiences helped the groups to understand the different environments that each experience.

♦ An LEA worker operating a mobile within a school catchment area organised a youth exchange to northern Spain. With part-funding from the Youth Exchange Centre, a group of 12 young people organised a ferry crossing and itinerary to visit youth clubs in rural settings using a converted furniture van as a base. The return leg involved young people staying with families back in England. One result was that in the following year some of the young people felt confident enough to take summer jobs in Spain.

INEQUALITY OF PROVISION

The Issues

One of the consequences of isolation experienced by young people is that in many cases their numbers are not sufficient for them to create the demand that their urban counterparts can exert on youth work providers by sheer weight of vocal numbers. It is on this basis that villages can frequently languish without any youth provision or where young people may have to accept second best facilities and unimaginative activities. Market forces ensure that resources are directed at the needs of the majority of consumers. Those on the margins have needs that will remain unmet unless youth work providers make explicit decisions to redress inequalities of provision on the basis of rights and entitlements. Some of the factors affecting the range and equality of rural youth provision therefore are:

♦ remoteness of youth work decision makers from rural consumers;

♦ the extra effort required to provide an adequate standard of youth work and youth facilities in rural areas may lead to inaction;

♦ the need to justify the allocation of resources by numbers of users and immediate pay off may reduce the priority of rural work;

- difficulty in challenging local power structures which may be hostile;
- lack of understanding of rural issues by agencies with a predominantly urban outlook; and
- the apparent lack of immediacy of rural problems.

Youth Work Responses

Appropriate youth work responses may encompass the following:
- all youth work providers with a national brief assessing the quality of their responses to rural needs in terms of creating explicit policies and monitoring practice;
- local youth work providers looking at funding arrangements which accept the relative costs of urban and rural work and build in elements of rural weighting;
- specialist rural development posts in both statutory and voluntary organisations;
- networking of staff to maintain a rural lobby within a local youth service; and
- national lobbying by countrywide groupings of rural youth work staff – for example, through Rural Impetus, local action groups, support groups.

Practice Examples

♦ In 1989, the Duke of Edinburgh's Award scheme received funding from the Prince Edward's Special Projects Group to expand the take up of the Award scheme in rural areas. Seventeen rural projects were established – eight in England, five in Scotland, three in Wales and one in Northern Ireland. Key aspects of the promotion were access to the Award by those with different needs, recruitment and training of adult volunteers, increase in local publicity, telephone support networks and mobile provision. The approach has been particularly successful in England in deep rural and fenland areas. A network of local village coordinators was recruited, few with any previous youth work experience and three rural committees

established, coordinating and promoting the scheme with contacts in all schools in the deep rural area.

This initiative was a conscious effort to open up opportunities to young people who were previously shut out from participating through logistical problems and to link them to adult volunteers in their own community. Those volunteers could provide advice and help to young people with a clear framework and support structure from the Award, potentially breaking down social barriers at the same time.

♦ The Scoutreach Development Programme aims to extend and support Scouting within communities and among social groups and cultures where take up is historically low. Projects can be registered if they expect to use innovative methods which require specific rules to be waived or amended, and experimental methods to provide activities and programmes.

In a fenland district, initial research suggested that Scouting could be developed in a particular village. Young people were contacted over a widely scattered area and adult interest assessed. The benefits of Scouting were promoted locally to parents and young people. Permission was granted for the Scout troop to provide for both young men and young women with a flexible structure reflecting the realities of numbers available and the working hours and availability of adult volunteers. The scheme provided opportunities for both young people and adults to take part in activities and develop skills not previously available to them or otherwise discounted because of logistical difficulties.

VISIBILITY

The Issues

Young people growing up in a rural area will tend to be highly visible to the adult community – perhaps as the child of 'known' local parents or labelled as the children of newcomers. Either way, many rural communities will be fierce in their expectations and harsh in expressing disapproval over any young person who steps outside the norm. Rural young people are likely to experience:

- close and potentially claustrophobic links with family, extended family and friends who live locally;
- involvement of family and family friends in most social activities;
- limits to mobility because of land use and ownership;
- few gathering places out of public view;
- evident disapproval from adults perceiving them to be 'hanging around' and 'up to no good' – attitudes often determined by the media concerning young people and crime, drugs, sexuality;
- difficulty in gaining confidential access to local services – especially on health matters; and
- labelling by the behaviour of family, older or younger siblings or peer group.

Youth Work Responses

An important task for youth work in a rural area is to reduce the visibility factor – either to find ways to counter the over-exposure of young people to public gaze or to lessen the sense of always being in the company of people who will feedback what you say or do directly to your parents. Youth work can:

- widen young people's relationships with adults;
- tackle the views of local people and harness their concerns;
- help locate or create appropriate provision that will meet the needs of young people and the adult community at the same time;
- create opportunities for young people to meet each other and talk to other adults in confidence; and
- offer a range of activities reducing the spiral of boredom, over-exposure and labelling

and offer positive experience of involvement and responsibility.

Practice Examples

♦ Youth workers in a West Midlands location organised a nine-week course called Choices, designed to encourage young people in a village to develop their leadership skills in decision making and planning, and to promote the sharing of ideas and contact with new friends. The content included sessions on self-image and self-esteem, the power of roles, needs, power in society, relationships with family and other adults, aggression, conflict and personal life histories. Methods used included icebreakers, brainstorming, small group work and working in pairs.

The course was successful, with many young people taking on greater responsibility in their local youth clubs or participating in a more positive matter. As a result local adults began to see the young people in a different light – as young adults with skills and a potential contribution to village life.

♦ An East Midlands CVYS established a project to target villages with no existing youth work provision. The hope was to mobilise adult support, to help young people to organise themselves and to reduce antagonism because of young people's visibility.

The worker appointed to the project started by locating adults who were concerned about the numbers of young people hanging around their village. By helping to convince people that something could be done, premises were located in a number of villages, committees formed and equipment loaned to get clubs started.

Where clubs are now operating successfully local young people recall saying: 'Before the project I always thought no-one would want to know us.' And adults now involved say: 'Before this I never had any time for the kids in this village – I always thought they were up to no good ...'

NEGATIVITY

The Issues

In rural communities negativity towards young people is often expressed by locals and incomers alike. Local adults mistrust the challenge they perceive young people to be making to the status quo while many incomers will harbour a negativity borne out of having moved to a rural area seeking to escape what they see as the urban phenomenon of an over-powerful youth culture. Rural young people will experience negativity through:

◆ adults defending their territory – the village hall, the pub, the sports pitch;

◆ being caught in the crossfire between sometimes different needs of members of the established community and incomers;

◆ the (almost) inevitability of adults' needs prevailing;

◆ the difficulty of meeting the needs of rural adults let alone young people's needs;

◆ lingering frustration at the local community's inability to meet its own needs because of the declining economic and social viability of many rural communities; and

◆ not-in-my-back-yard syndrome – begrudging acknowledgment of need, but no provision next to my cottage please!

Youth Work Responses

Youth workers can act as advocates for young people in conflict with the local community. They do this at both a personal and a structural level – supporting young people's rights to association and their legitimate access to services that will meet their needs. Capitalising on local concern is important – encouraging adults to begin to act, to become involved and to press for local action to meet the needs of all parties. This can be achieved by:

◆ identifying ways to demonstrate young people's positive contribution to the local community;

◆ involving adults and young people together in looking for ways to improve local facilities;

◆ using youth work and community work skills to mobilise public support;

◆ taking action step by step – building confidence for further action by young people and adults alike;

◆ using curriculum materials to explore why adults find young people's behaviour threatening; and

◆ youth workers acting as public advocates for the legitimate needs of young people.

Practice Example

◆ Two part-time sessional workers from the local authority worked over a six month period with young people from an existing rural club to improve its image, to involve young people in their local community in a positive way and to increase the involvement of local adults. Work began by looking at ways to start the project off – suggestions included undertaking a survey of local adults, taking part in a village fundraising event, developing a newsletter/magazine and finding ways to produce more sophisticated publicity.

A group of 12 young people between the ages of 14 and 18 began meeting once a week to plan and allocate tasks. The group was evenly mixed by gender, but demonstrated a wide range of awareness and confidence. Over the six months the club and its standing in the community were transformed. A local firm was talked into donating timber and materials. A local builder gave his time to advise and assist with improvements to the building. Display boards were built, storage cupboards created, and the club grounds improved. Improvements in ambience and ownership for the project led to the young people involved challenging other club members' attitudes and behaviour, resulting in constructive debate about young people's public image.

A more positive profile in the community

led to new relationships between the club and the local sheltered housing scheme and ultimately to the creation of a new and supportive management committee consisting of several local people previously uninvolved with youth work.

5B
Identity

For young people living in rural areas, the issues around identity and stereotyping are fundamental to their understanding of themselves, their abilities, potential and worth. This section examines the way in which the issues of personal isolation and visibility explored previously in Section 5A (pages 51-61) may be experienced by different groups of young people. It explains how many young people may feel more visible because their sense of identity differs from their peers, more isolated because they have few friends who share their experiences, and yet more vulnerable to stereotyping from the local community which may display a range of prejudices.

LOCAL IDENTITY

The Issues

Many young people growing up in rural areas experience fundamental difficulties around their sense of identity with the place in which they are being brought up. They may be aware from an early age that their place and activities do not signify very much in the national youth culture. This can engender feelings of inferiority. At the same time they may find that their village and countryside hold very different meanings for hordes of visitors who make use of it for recreational, sporting, educational or cultural purposes or for spiritual uplift. This may result in very ambiguous feelings about their home area including:

♦ a sense of very few people sharing their understanding of the meaning and history of their geographical location for their family and neighbours;

♦ a simultaneous attachment to familiar surroundings, but intense desire to be somewhere else more lively;

♦ a sense of intrusion from visitors who may be needed as a source of income but simultaneously resented;

♦ a resentment on behalf of indigenous young people of some incomers who have the wealth and influence to impose their view of the world on the community and control change;

♦ a sense of loss on behalf of incomers of previous surroundings, friendships; and

♦ potential rivalries between both groups.

Youth Work Responses

Addressing these very deepseated issues may well be one of the hardest tasks for youth workers who themselves may be incomers from urban or other rural locations. There may, however, be very little difference between these two backgrounds in terms of how they are perceived by young people. Youth workers can:

♦ get young people to articulate their feelings about their home and locality;

♦ encourage exchange events which may allow young people to make realistic comparisons between rural and urban activities and centres;

♦ host events which allow young people to share with others their own vision of the countryside;

♦ encourage activities which enable young people to discover something unique about themselves and their locality; and

♦ through political education, enable young people to make their views known about decisions affecting their locality.

Practice Examples

♦ A group of young people from the rural East Midlands was encouraged to research the history of a local prisoner of war camp which had existed in their area. Representatives from local villages formed a team to video the camp's history. Former inmates who had stayed on after the war in the area were interviewed and shared photographs, and local people also contributed their memories. The completed film was shown in local village halls before being deposited in the library archive. Young people acquired skills in film making, developed greater international awareness which was followed up by a youth exchange to Germany and created a unique record of genuine local history that was previously unknown to them.

♦ Following a performance of a visiting theatre group to a village hall, a group of workers and young people were inspired to look at local history from the perspective of villagers. By exploring the memories of young people themselves, of older siblings, family and friends, the young people gained the confidence to interview villagers about their experiences in the 1950s, during the war and as far back as the 1920s. This gave a new perspective on the village itself, its landmarks and its place in history, creating a sense of pride in where they lived.

WORK WITH GIRLS AND YOUNG WOMEN

The Issues

In many rural areas girls and young women may experience:

♦ stereotypical expectations concerning their role, responsibilities and likely future work from their parents and other adults;

♦ isolation and difficult transport logistics restricting face-to-face contacts with best friends;

♦ safety issues and parental protectiveness towards girls limiting the amount of independent travel and activities feasible if they need to rely on parents or other adults for lifts, or public transport;

♦ limited access to contraception or advice concerning their sexuality and sexual health;

♦ village youth clubs with male oriented activities which they may or may not attend, depending on their relationships with the boys and young men involved;

♦ part-time or voluntary youth workers who may not recognise their need for separate provision and experiences or be uncomfortable about making a case for it;

♦ little access to female rural youth workers because of the difficulties in getting the work supported and recognised;

♦ few activities of interest to older young women, so little involvement;

♦ few chances of advice, support, avoidance, escape or refuge from incest and other forms of sexual and physical abuse;

♦ responsibility for ageing parents or young siblings in the absence of other sources of support;

♦ extreme reaction to the local environment involving either a desire to escape totally into an urban centre, or a marked reluctance to move or travel away from home at all; and

♦ little recognition likely or specialist help available for any sexual abuse or other sexual experiences.

Young mothers are likely to experience:

♦ difficult access to health care;

♦ reduced childminding facilities, outside the immediate family;

♦ punitive attitudes to one-parent families from the local community;

♦ increased isolation and responsibility;

♦ low income;

♦ accommodation difficulties or added pressure on overcrowded family home;

♦ reduced opportunities for leisure activities that are either affordable or logistically possible; and

♦ reduced privacy in relationships.

Youth Work Responses

To address these issues youth workers can provide:

♦ a safe girls-only environment in which a group can meet and interact;

♦ a programme which addresses issues of concern to the girls and young women;

♦ access to individual experiences which widen horizons, boost confidence and redress inequalities;

♦ activities which address the powerlessness and inequality inherent in women's experience of rural life; and

♦ opportunities for young mothers to meet for mutual support and begin to address their particular needs.

Practice Examples

♦ A network of women workers in the Southwest established a support group for young mothers. The aim has been to encourage mutual support and to empower young parents through confidence building, assertiveness training and developing group trust. Information has been offered about legal rights, parenting skills, health issues and educational opportunities.

The group balances discussion with activities covering a wide range of topics. To enable discussion to take place the group has used various games and exercises to develop trust. It has undertaken work around drug misuse, especially prescribed barbiturates and cigarette smoking. Sessions usually operate with a crèche so that the young mothers can pay full attention to the agendas. Such discussion has been balanced with activities – dance, massage and relaxation, swimming trips and picnics.

♦ A northern rural county youth service set up a group for young mothers living in the rural hinterland of a market town. Contact was made through health visitors and a core group of 12 young parents established. Activities have included canoeing, homeopathy, reflexology, crafts, discussion on sexuality using curriculum materials such as *The Grapevine Game,* and

organised trips. As an offshoot, a six-week child development course has been organised on child development issues. The group is self-supporting through fundraising events.

♦ A group of ten young women with children from the rural areas around a town in the far Southwest has met regularly with youth workers and developed a peer group model of education and mutual support. They have covered themes of violence, abuse, stress, contraception, mental health and child development, organised special events such as the county leg of the National Pop Quiz and run county-wide training events for other women.

♦ Youth workers in the West Midlands established a sexual harassment, abuse, attack, rape project to help young victims. A number of young survivors are receiving long-term counselling help.

♦ A group of eight 14 to 15-year-old young women has participated in a peer education project in the Southwest as part of a national initiative by the Department of Health, funded by the local health authority to reduce the numbers of teenage pregnancies. The young women, working with a part-time youth worker and a volunteer, are empowered to help each other and become better informed on sexuality and health issues.

They meet in a local town, but live in the surrounding rural area. They have worked on sexual health, AIDS, contraception, reproductive rights and communication skills. They have made a video of their work which has been shown to adult professionals. Similar groups are planned in other areas of the county.

♦ Many rural youth services have addressed the need of girls and young women for time to themselves to meet and consider issues of special relevance to them. Since much rural youth provision caters for all ages and both sexes, this has often necessitated using existing centres on other nights or bringing young women together in other centres, or meeting on mobiles. A wide range of issues has been tackled including health, sexuality, outdoor activities, developing self-confidence, unfamiliar activities and experiences, arts work, discussion, peer education and support. Youth workers have been able to offer much individual support and counselling.

WORK WITH BOYS AND YOUNG MEN

The Issues

Boys and young men may experience some of the following gender specific issues as a result of living in rural areas:

♦ attitudes and expectations from the local community based on the long-standing reputation of their fathers and other male family members;
♦ traditional models of masculinity with an emphasis on hard work and physical strength;
♦ traditional socialisation into male sexual roles – breadwinner, disciplinarian, fighter;
♦ experience of adult women, usually only in conventional roles;
♦ restricted choice of partners of both sexes;
♦ feelings of extreme territoriality regarding their own locality;
♦ expectation that either the reputation or physical integrity of amenities in the locality will need to be defended against other hostile local males, by force if necessary;
♦ dislike of seasonal visitors and occasional hostility towards them;
♦ hostility towards people of different race, cultural or sexual orientation;
♦ male peer relationships likely to be long-

standing and close with the potential for both desirable and undesirable influences on behaviour;
♦ considerable pressure to work in family business with difficult choices to be made about future opportunities elsewhere;
♦ reputation gained in childhood and adolescence may persist for a long time into adulthood;
♦ injury from farm machinery (accessible from an early age) and personal or borrowed transport driven late at night in hazardous conditions; and
♦ little recognition likely or specialist help available for sexual abuse or other personal sexual experiences.

As fathers, young men may experience:

♦ being trapped into a relationship with no real choice through lack of potential partners;
♦ frustration at inability to take on responsibilities adequately through lack of access to independent employment and housing;
♦ tendency to reproduce traditional attitudes and behaviour towards women and parenthood;
♦ reluctance to give up existing limited social activities to share childcare;
♦ separation from partner due to substantial distances from education, training or a job with a long-term future;
♦ inability to help with childcare due to long hours commuting; and
♦ low wages reinforcing the poverty cycle compounded by likelihood of the mother being unable to work through lack of affordable childcare.

Youth Work Responses

Youth work with boys and young men, as well as addressing issues arising out of the needs of all rural adolescents, can tackle deep seated male attitudes towards women and outsiders, for example, by:

♦ challenging conventional attitudes to

masculinity;

- ♦ challenging conventional attitudes to women;
- ♦ fostering cooperative activities with occupants of neighbouring villages and towns;
- ♦ widening horizons;
- ♦ introducing a wider range of activities and leisure/recreation pursuits; and
- ♦ challenging racist, sexist and homophobic attitudes.

Youth work responses to young fathers can:

- ♦ explore feelings about fatherhood and individual's relationships with their own fathers through groupwork;
- ♦ foster supportive relationships with their partners as mothers;
- ♦ offer information about child development and childcare;
- ♦ enhance understanding about stress and potential dangers of physical abuse; and
- ♦ work strategically to improve housing opportunities for young couples.

Practice Examples

♦ Over time a male youth worker in the Home Counties had established a good enough relationship with a group of young men in a village youth club to respond to their discussions and anxieties about sexuality. Informal discussion in the course of normal youth work led to the worker and a group of ten young men aged 15 to 17 examining issues of sexuality, gender and masculinity once a week for a year in a special session which was separate from the main youth club evening. They used a wide range of games, exercises and role plays to explore the issues, resulting in a significant impact on both attitudes and behaviour.

♦ The issue of young men's territoriality was tackled by youth workers in the Home Counties through the development of an Arts Youth League. This was specifically designed to involve mixed groups – young men and young women – in non-competitive events involving participants from villages with an historical antipathy to each other. Through the activities of the League, Asian and African-Caribbean groups from town-based clubs also visited local villages when they hosted events – places where they might otherwise have been made unwelcome. The learning gained helped engender less aggressive behaviour and less overt racism.

♦ A local branch of the National Association of Boys' Clubs – Clubs for Young People in the Northwest undertook some detached work with a group of eight or so young men aged 15 to 17 who had been barred from their local village youth club because of their behaviour. They ran a programme one night a week for two months and then moved to a fortnightly meeting until the group gradually dissolved.

The group members had to agree a contract about behaving responsibly at the start and to commit themselves to the group. They took part in some activities designed to build trust and team work and were able to visit other youth centres in the surrounding district and take part in their programme.

The initiative by this voluntary youth organisation helped to meet a need which the statutory sector could not resource, and enabled some positive work to be done with some disaffected young men who might otherwise have got into further trouble.

WORK WITH GAY AND LESBIAN YOUNG PEOPLE

The Issues

Young people who are attracted to others of the same sex experience particular difficulty in tight knit rural areas and may experience:

- ♦ lack of understanding of their feelings through absence of positive role models and impartial information or sympathetic advice;

- little or no access to specialist magazines or literature and no chance to buy or order anonymously;
- homophobic attitudes in the local community – harmful where sexual orientation is concealed; where it is not, giving rise to personal abuse, bullying or assault;
- little recognition likely or specialist help available for sexual abuse and other personal sexual experiences;
- reduced numbers of potential partners in surrounding area;
- absence of safe space in which to socialise;
- loneliness and isolation;
- despair;
- lack of support from heterosexual male or female peers;
- adoption of heterosexual partnership to avoid loneliness and isolation; and
- difficulties in coming out to parents in tight knit communities.

Youth Work Responses

Youth workers need to provide a range of responses to address these needs but may be subject to restrictions – actual or self-imposed – on the type of work they can do. Progress is likely to be slow and painstaking with many setbacks. Examples of responses include:

- challenging homophobia among indigenous young people and their communities;
- developing trust between workers and young people in which self-disclosure may be possible;
- supporting and advising young people who come out;
- raising the issue in their authority or agency so that there is explicit support for their work; and
- helping young people to make contact with gay and lesbian lines.

Practice Examples

- A youth worker employed by an inter-agency group in a rural centre of population in the Home Counties identified a need for support for isolated young gay and lesbian people in rural areas. After working in a gay centre to try to understand the issues better, she made contact with a local group and discussed their needs. They were then able to form themselves into a voluntary group keeping her as a consultant.

  A telephone helpline was the first identified need and they were helped to negotiate use of an existing gay and lesbian switchboard in the area for two hours once a week to provide a counselling and advice service for young people. The second need identified was for a safe place to meet. Funding was obtained to make use of voluntary premises in the nearest town to operate a drop-in session on Saturdays. This provides a central point for young lesbians and gays to find support.

- A youth worker in the Home Counties organised a six-week course in a rural market town on homophobia with a group of twelve or more young men aged 15 to 18 using the B Team's *Man's World* game and other resources. A questionnaire was used to help identify the issues.

- A small group of young people in the West Midlands had recently discussed sexuality and gender. The opportunity to go to a play about the rent boy scene in the nearest large city generated wide discussion.

  The outing was a considerable success and enabled previously stereotypical attitudes to be swept aside. There has been a significant increase in tolerance and understanding of issues around gender, relationships, sexual orientation and prejudice. Experiences were shared with friends and figured prominently in discussions months later. It also legitimised honest discussions around sexual orientation, often a difficult and sensitive area for young people to confront.

TACKLING RURAL RACISM

The Issues

A very common assertion is that racism is not a problem in rural areas because very few Black people* have chosen to settle there. The justification for this has always been dubious. Attitudes will have been formed in the absence of first-hand experience of people from a different culture. The lack of contact is also likely to foster more extreme and unfounded prejudices. This has to be addressed in youth work, by direct support to the small numbers of Black young people who do live in the area and by equipping white young people from the local rural population to live and work in multicultural Britain – especially if they move away from their home to urban settings for employment and housing.

White Young People

White young people are likely to display:
- reduced awareness of different cultures;
- stereotypical prejudice directed against 'different' young people;
- reluctance to expose themselves to new experiences and friendships; and
- pressure from family and peers to maintain uninformed potentially prejudicial attitudes.

Black Young People

Black young people in rural areas are likely to experience:
- extreme visibility because of their small numbers;
- few or no peers within easy reach;
- attitudes and behaviour ranging from ignorance and prejudice to violence and harassment from the local community;
- attitudes of hostility or 'novelty value' within their schools from pupils and possibly covert racism from teachers;

* *The National Youth Agency works with a definition of the word Black which includes members of African, African-Caribbean, Asian and other communities which are oppressed by racism.*

- frequent involvement in family business in some cases with few opportunities for socialising with local young people; and
- considerable travel in order to take part in religious or cultural events in larger centres of population.

Youth Work Responses

The youth work task on this issue is likely to be both sensitive and demanding and involve:
- identification of Black young people who may be in need of support;
- alerting senior managers to issues and the need for clear policies and strategies;
- support to Black young people in a way that is culturally sensitive and addresses their special concerns;
- challenging prejudiced attitudes of local young people;
- organising exchanges and experiences which widen horizons and develop first-hand local young people's knowledge of Black cultures and the problems Black individuals encounter; and
- personal recognition of the extent of racism, its manifestations and the range of groups which experience it.

Practice Examples

♦ Youth workers in an upland area had taken part in a racism awareness weekend which had left them feeling that they should introduce their young people to Black workers and young people from other areas. A joint weekend was planned with white and Black young people from a local town. Activities such as music, drama and sound recording were shared together with rock climbing, canoeing, netball and self-defence. Friendships were forged, joint visits between youth clubs organised and a second weekend based around music took place.

Following this exchange a mixed group of white, Asian and African-Caribbean young people from a wide geographical area overcame the logistical barriers and set themselves up as a

Rural Youth Link Group. They set about organising a youth exchange with a multiracial French group, raised the funds, made the arrangements and made the exchange a success. Having met each other once, the young people were enthusiastic enough to carry the project forward by their own efforts. People of vastly different backgrounds whom geography and all the other constraints of a rural area normally keep apart, got together and created friendships, breaking down the barriers that they previously assumed to exist between them.

♦ A youth worker from a rural bus project in a former mining area worked with a group of ten young people from a village who had been meeting for a year. As part of an issue-based programme she used a curriculum pack about the life of Anne Frank to address issues of racism and oppression in relation to Black people. The combination of the worker needing to learn the best way of approaching the issues and the group learning to trust each other meant that the programme took time to get established, but this became a thought-provoking piece of work culminating in a visit to a Black centre in a nearby city.

♦ A rural worker organised a group visit from a village in the rural patch where he worked. It involved a minibus journey with a mixed group into the city 20 miles away to use the facilities of a leisure centre where the group was going to be involved in inter-club competitions. The journey meant travelling through a part of the city with many Asian shops and businesses. As they reached this point of the journey the older lads began verbally abusing passers-by, taunting, jeering and mooning at pedestrians and drivers.

The worker stopped the minibus, dealt with the immediate behaviour, but more importantly used the incident as a stepping-off point for the use of curriculum materials and discussions to explore attitudes, behaviour and how uninformed prejudice leads to racism. Later work back at the club included looking at the rise of fascism, the activities of the British National Party (BNP) and the growth of racial incidents in urban areas.

WORK WITH TRAVELLERS

The Issues

Young people who belong to a range of itinerant groups or who have adopted an itinerant lifestyle and are labelled New Age travellers, encounter particular difficulties and prejudices.

Travellers
♦ may have limited traditional acceptance within local rural communities but face hostility from many incomers and widespread stereotyping;
♦ will have a range of occupations including fairground staff, bargees, antique traders;
♦ will have little neutral contact with local young people and be likely to face hostility in youth clubs;
♦ may have little opportunity for young women to socialise because of strict role demarcation entailing extensive domestic and childcare responsibilities;
♦ may be suspicious of outsiders (including youth workers) because of hassles from authority figures;
♦ experience problems accessing local schools and consequent literacy and learning problems;
♦ face playground hostility; and
♦ face potential health problems because of lack of regular access to health care.

New Age Travellers
♦ face particular hostility from both traditional rural communities and incomers;
♦ lack legitimate access to range of local services;
♦ few local advocates;
♦ face potential drug and health problems; and

♦ have ambiguous relationships with local young people.

Youth Work Responses

Youth workers may face considerable local opposition when seeking to extend services to this group and will need clear policies in place and explicit managerial support. Responses can:

♦ address deep-rooted prejudice in the host community;

♦ promote the integration of traveller young people into the local community while acknowledging their chosen lifestyle;

♦ address the particular needs of traveller girls and young women; and

♦ use advocacy and mediation skills to reconcile antagonists.

Practice Examples

♦ Youth workers have undertaken extensive work with young people involved in the travelling fairground and English gypsy culture in rural sites in the East Midlands. In one county a specialist mobile worker initially made contact with fairground families helping them get access to local services, involving young people in local activities and promoting use of the mobile youth centre. Targeted work with young women was also undertaken.

The mobile provided opportunities for young gypsy travellers to become involved in activities on the bus and on outings in which they would not otherwise be able to participate. Developing from this initial contact, a group of young travellers decided to create a video which would help develop a greater awareness of gypsy culture, the discrimination they face in everyday life and the changes which have taken place over the past few years.

Through this work young travellers have been able to challenge the prejudices of the settled community, and youth workers have been able to address some of the aspects of traveller life which restrict the young people's experiences.

A women's caravan project has now been established which works primarily with women aged 14 to 21 who would otherwise have little opportunity to meet, to discuss issues or to travel off-site together.

♦ Youth workers in a coastal hinterland area on the Northeast coast developed a traveller project based in a market town on one evening a week at a local youth club. Initially, the project was attended by young males only, but visits by the workers to the traveller site succeeded in reducing anxieties, to the extent that many young women began to attend. The young people have increasingly grown in confidence and are now taking an active part in running the programmes, alongside the regular club users. Youth workers are learning constantly about the life, attitudes and values of the traveller culture, and are increasingly able to educate and involve non-traveller members in developing a better understanding of that culture.

♦ A mobile supported by the youth service and operating in a Southern downland area provides a service to traveller families, offering a facility to girls not attending normal secondary schools. The project involves both teachers and youth workers – teachers offering tuition including literacy and numeracy, with arts and crafts work provided by the bus workers.

DISABILITY

The Issues

Within rural areas, the experiences of disabled young people because of their impairments can be compounded by increased isolation, problems of access to services and prevailing attitudes. Attention has to be given both to disabled young people and to the attitudes of non-disabled young people.

Disabled young people in rural areas may experience:

- isolation and separation from peers with similar disabilities;
- a lack of opportunity to build friendships with local children and young people – especially if placed within special education, as long journeys to special schools are likely to require early starts and tiredness at the end of the day;
- reduced access to local community buildings and facilities;
- shortage of accessible local activities in the summer holidays when they could benefit most from social contact with local young people;
- lack of information about and access to integrated clubs or activity sessions such as swimming/Physically Handicapped and Able Bodied (PHAB) clubs, which are likely to be located in towns;
- untrained full-time, part-time and voluntary staff who lack experience in integrating disabled young people and are thus ultra-cautious – perhaps expecting parental presence as support both at evening sessions and during trips away;
- public transport which is either non-existent or impossible to use, with alternatives such as taxis likely to be expensive;
- local provision which claims to be integrated, but where disabled young people are segregated;
- the prospect of verbal abuse and bullying:
  - from peers at integrated schools;
  - from peers in local village or town; or
  - from peers at youth clubs and groups;
- parental control over leisure activities because of dependence on them for transport and support; and
- reduced participation in local activities because of parents':

- fears about safety/bullying;
- anxiety about levels of training on the part of staff;
- embarrassment about the nature of the young person's disability; and
- philosophical tensions concerning integrated versus specialist provision.

Young people in rural communities who are non-disabled may express:

- some familiarity with individual disabled young people living locally in their village;
- stereotyping of local families with disabled young people; and
- unacceptable behaviour towards disabled young people ranging from exclusion and bullying to practical jokes and limited acceptance and integration into social groups.

Youth Work Responses

Youth workers can:

- challenge unhelpful attitudes and practices in statutory and voluntary agencies;
- disseminate information about all youth service provision widely reaching disabled young people and their parents;
- provide summer holiday schemes with integrated provision;
- address over-protectiveness on the part of parents;
- review and take action on the accessibility of youth facilities;
- ensure all staff receive training on disability awareness;
- provide explicit support and training to part-time and voluntary staff in village youth provision to assist them to integrate young people with disabilities more successfully;
- enable individual young people to share their experiences of disability with each other and to organise collective action to make local services more responsive; and
- enable disabled young people to choose what they want to be involved in whether it is segregated or integrated.

Practice Examples

♦ A senior PHAB group based in a town in a coastal hinterland in the Northeast is attended by disabled and non-disabled young people aged between 13 and 30. The group leader is a wheelchair user. Activities have included the production of a video of the club, its members and activities produced mainly by club members with little professional help. Group members take part in a wide range of activities such as swimming, uni-hock (indoor hockey) and table tennis. Senior member training is available which enables members of the Junior PHAB club to progress and take responsibility in the senior club.

In 1993, the National PHAB organisation received funding from the DFE to work on issues affecting disabled young people in rural areas. The project intends to look at ways of supporting village club leaders to integrate local disabled young people into youth provision.

♦ A youth service in the West Midlands organised a youth exchange to Amsterdam for ten non-disabled and ten disabled people from a rural district, linking up with a Dutch youth group of a similar composition.

All the young people shared the experience of a safe environment which enabled them to experience independence, self-reliance and new experiences such as a flight in a light aircraft. Friendships between people in the group have been maintained and a return visit by the Dutch group took place soon afterwards.

♦ A youth club in a small town in the East Midlands with a membership including young people from rural villages arranged sessions on oppression, society and prejudice. The work included meetings on disability awareness using a video to prompt discussion. For a later session, the group invited a disabled youth worker to attend, challenging some of the young people's assumptions about the skills and abilities of disabled people.

CLASS AND POWER

The Issues

The operation and maintenance of the class system in many rural areas may be far more explicit than in larger centres of population where power may be shared among a number of competing groups. Traditionally, landowners had privileged access to decision making at a whole range of local levels – parish and district councils, school governors, the Bench of Magistrates, local management committees and county council structures. Local professionals, such as clergy and school teachers, would be involved.

The indigenous population often had little power beyond their economic function, but might experience some ritual transfer of resources on set occasions. Close face-to-face relationships sometimes cut across class barriers.

In many places the balance of power has not effectively changed but new players have come on the scene. Many new landowners have no local ties but operate their businesses on a purely economic basis with little regard to social consequences. Wealthy incomers constitute a new group which may have the political skills to influence decision making in their locality and set the tone for future developments.

But the reality for many young people, born and bred in a rural area may be little different from that experienced by their parents and grandparents:

♦ powerlessness – taking the form of identification with an area, but being shut out of any effective participation in decisions affecting it;
♦ a feeling of alienation from the values and outlook of prominent members of the community who control local land use and institutions;
♦ low or nil expectations of beneficial change;
♦ danger of stereotyping by local figures of authority;

- cultural expectations to accept the current social order;
- overt personal power exerted by heads of families;
- decisions by incoming families to move to an area without taking account of effects on children;
- national politics dominated by urban issues; and
- distance from regional/national decision-making apparatus.

Youth Work Responses

Youth work can offer many ways of enabling young people to feel included in decisions that affect their lives. Such work can begin by ensuring young people have a voice in local provision – the running of the village youth club as a starting point – but can also easily provide opportunities for breaking down class barriers and accessing political processes on a larger scale. Youth work can offer:

- opportunities for active involvement and participation in the running of youth projects from simple representation to total control;
- involvement in local youth councils – young people's organisations designed to give voice to young people's concerns;
- local youth committees – shadow groups to council committees or committees with a remit (and sometimes budget) of their own;
- involvement in local youth work organisations with national structures – for example:
  - Youth Clubs UK national members committee;
  - URC and other church youth committees;
  - British Youth Council (BYC); and
  - Young Farmers' Clubs;
- involvement in parliamentary lobbies and national participation projects – for example, NYA's Vox Pops;
- opportunity to explore the history of a local area and its power structures;
- action groups on local issues:

- against cuts and closures affecting local youth services, schools, or hospitals; or
- environmental action;
- action groups on national issues:
  - fundraising for charities; or
  - Sleep Out Week; and
- action groups on international issues:
  - political prisoners; or
  - famine, disaster relief.

Youth workers' responses to these issues have to be highly sensitive. Youth workers have to:

- recognise and analyse the local power structure and identify points of influence;
- operate and negotiate with local powerbrokers with the interests of young people in mind;
- introduce elements of participation and political education into the curriculum which are geared to relevant and accessible issues;
- introduce activities which ensure that inequalities and barriers to the participation of various groups are addressed; and
- ensure parity of adequate provision in both urban and rural areas.

Practice Examples

♦ An area youth worker in the West Midlands identified the potential interest of local councillors in exploring ways for parish committees to hear young people's views on local topics. For the worker, aiming to help develop young people's skills to take part in community affairs, this provided an opportunity for devising a scheme to help develop an understanding of participation, decision-making and local power, to help develop personal confidence and to explore the workings and responsibilities of parish and town councils.

By working with the county-wide parish council association and the county youth service, a training day was set up which brought together councillors and young people to explore their different experiences and understandings of the work of parishes, their powers, and parishes' ability to respond to the needs of young people. Meeting on the neutral ground of a county training venue, the day sparked off a number of developments back in individual parishes including ideas for youth parish councils. Many of the young people went back to their local communities and organisations determined to act on the information they received and the new skills they discovered.

♦ A youth worker, based at a local school in the Home Counties, became aware that young people in a rural area wanted to do more for their village and have more of their needs recognised by the adult community.

A youth parish council was suggested and the local parish council was invited to attend a meeting with young people to explore the idea. The meeting was well attended and resulted in the parish council supporting the formation of a youth parish council and offering to help finance the first few meetings. The two groups exchange minutes and agendas to ensure communication between them.

The group has been involved in fundraising, recycling and environmental projects and more general youth work events. It has been undertaking projects to heighten its profile around the village, such as cleaning the village brook. Meetings continue every other week and representatives from the Rural Community Council as well as the youth worker are invited at regular intervals.

INCOMERS

The Issues

The population shift from urban to some rural areas in recent years has run in parallel with a continuing but fundamental depopulation of the countryside in other areas. By and large the movement has consisted of a shift of elements of the indigenous population into urban areas to find work, while rural areas have seen an increase in a middle-class population either retiring to the country, choosing to bring up families there or able, with new technology, to sustain a working base within a country location.

The children of these incomers form a new group on the rural scene with particular needs and concerns of their own. Their experiences may include:
♦ potential separation by attitude, experience, wealth and outlook from their rural peers;
♦ lack of identification with a rural location;
♦ similar problems of isolation and lack of access to leisure, special interests and friends as other young people, but on an individualised basis; and
♦ mutual hostility.

Youth Work Responses

Youth workers may not see incomers as being particularly in need or may assume that parents are able and willing to fund and organise social education experiences for their children. There may be hidden problems and difficulties, however, which sympathetic befriending may bring to light and skills and experiences which could be shared with local young people if existing barriers to contact could be surmounted. Youth workers can:
♦ assess the various groupings of young people within their patch and match their responses accordingly, without too many preconceptions of what these needs might be;
♦ take active steps to reduce tensions between indigenous young people and incomers; and
♦ design activities that enable incomers and local young people to share their experiences and to overcome the mutual mistrust that may be evident.

Practice Example

♦ A report from a rural community council in East Anglia identified some difficulty in integrating newcomers to the area into long-established rural communities. The town council of a market town in the county decided it would like to respond to this issue and set up a sub-group which included a youth officer with responsibility for community education – rural development.

It was decided to organise a day in which all the organisations in the town would put on a display of their activities and invite newcomers to attend. The local community hall was hired and there was a good response from organisations such as the Scouts, the Guide Association, St John Ambulance, local choirs, playgroups, Age Concern and many others. To publicise the event the group leafleted door-to-door on the new estates, used estate agents to contact people new to the area and included an article in the community newspaper.

The event was successful in attracting newcomers, including young people, who had an opportunity to make contact with groups which might be of interest to them. The event was of interest to local residents as well and also enabled members of local organisations to network with each other. A similar event held the following year was even more successful.

UNEMPLOYMENT

The Issues

Unemployed young people face particular difficulties in rural areas. Unemployed young people aged 17 and over:
- are highly visible;
- experience isolation from friends in a similar position;
- may face punitive attitudes and stereotyping from the local community, as well as from immediate family;
- have no access to the kind of subsidised recreation or support facilities which may be available to urban unemployed young people;
- find that the local jobcentre/social security office is in nearest town, difficult to check on a daily basis;
- find the cost of fares or personal transport a significant drain on benefits;
- experience intermittent employment/ unemployment status with seasonal work/odd jobs leading to hassles with tax/social security and lost benefit;
- find their parents having to provide greater economic support although may themselves be on low income;
- may feel greater obligation to help in family business to earn their keep;
- find that young women may form a 'hidden' unemployed sector through reabsorbtion into family responsibilities after school; and
- have little sense of viable future in the local area.

Youth Work Responses

Youth work responses can:
- link the unemployed to information about jobs and training opportunities;
- provide personal support;
- offer individual advocacy in the search for jobs/training opportunities;
- engage unemployed young people's hidden interests and skills;
- bring together other agencies – careers, jobcentres, libraries;
- offer assistance to access both leisure and training facilities; and
- work with training providers, and TECs, to mobilise appropriate training opportunities.

Practice Examples

♦ A Scout Association project in the Southwest, set up as an independent company in the early 1980s, uses a mobile for a number of community action initiatives including job clubs and training schemes. The trailer takes facilities, such as on-board telephones, faxes and information, to rural villages where unemployed young people are living.

♦ Telecottages offer a local accessible venue with high-tech equipment – fax, modems, word processors, teletext, and increasingly satellite links. Telecottages can offer access to up-to-date information about the job market, training places and offer help in preparing job applications, CVs and in developing office skills, publishing and computer skills. Access to actual work such as desktop publishing, design and graphics generation is also available which can be encouraged as either a home working task or be combined with return to work training.

♦ Workers operating from a converted ambulance in the West Midlands/Welsh borders offer advocacy and support to individual young people currently unemployed. Work includes helping with benefit problems, negotiating places with training providers and FE colleges, help with interview preparation and more personal support. The workers bring the range of situations they encounter to the attention of the appropriate organisation in order to influence future provision.

♦ A youth service in the Southwest organised an initiative to assist young unemployed people in rural areas to become more motivated to seek employment and enable them to get careers advice in their own locality. Youth workers set up day centres in four village halls on one or two evenings a week which attracted up to thirty young people in each centre. A travel allowance was included to enable workers to collect young people and bring them to the centres. Once there they took part in general recreation and other activities. This included setting up a workers' cooperative, making craft items and selling them.

The youth service arranged for the careers service to visit the centres once a fortnight, providing information and advice and it also, in one centre, paid for a telephone line to be

installed so that young people could ring employers. As well as running the sessions at the centres, the youth workers took part in outreach sessions, visiting the homes of young people and talking to their parents. This proved valuable in helping mothers and fathers understand the difficulty facing young people in finding employment and may have eased some of the family pressures on young people.

CRIME

The Issues

Recent crime statistics show that many rural areas are experiencing the greatest statistical increases in reported crime. For young people, however, being accused of a crime in a rural area may carry far different consequences than for their counterparts in urban areas and may lead to them not receiving just treatment. Young people from rural areas accused of offences may experience:
♦ long-standing family labelling with police and the local community;
♦ high visibility;
♦ high chances of being caught if guilty;
♦ long travelling times and considerable expense likely for visits to individuals in remand centres, secure units and prisons;
♦ practical problems in organising bail support or alternative to custody schemes because of transport difficulties;
♦ difficulty in getting access to adequate legal advice; and
♦ time consuming logistics for social workers/ probation officers to make home visits to gather information for pre-sentence reports.

Youth Work Responses

Rural youth workers may find they have a significant role to play in court cases. This could include:

- advocacy and support for the young person with the police at the point of arrest;
- support at court appearances;
- help in obtaining appropriate legal advice;
- support to families when visiting;
- personal visiting and help to maintain links with community;
- cooperation with other agencies in crime prevention schemes;
- diversion; and
- involvement in reparation and victim support schemes.

Workers also need to be alert to the growth in official crime prevention schemes such as Neighbourhood Watch and also the potential of direct action by local vigilantes. In either case, rural workers need to be prepared to be involved as advocates for young people and to support or counter action as appropriate.

Practice Examples

♦ A downland youth and community service is the lead agency in an inter-agency venture providing holiday playschemes across the county for a six-week period each summer. This provides a focus for young people who may be at risk of becoming involved in offending who are able to engage in more constructive activities during this high-risk period.

♦ A northern upland county operates a motorbike project which provides opportunities for young people under 22 to use facilities such as a flat oval track for novice riders, a woodland and water trail for trial bikes and a full motorcross track. Two-hour evening workshop sessions are held weekly. As the project is targeted at young people in a predominantly rural area, travelling times and distances can be substantial. The project is used by youth service groups, but also accepts referrals from probation and social services of young people who have been guilty of auto offences, although membership policy is increasingly cautious.

♦ A youth work team in the Home Counties used its links with the probation service to provide an opportunity to place a 19–year-old man at a village youth club to fulfil a community service order. He completed his programme and was well liked and supported by leaders, committee and young people alike. With their encouragement he has continued to work at the club as a volunteer, despite having to arrive an hour early because of a minimal bus service. The Management Committee reimburses his fare. He has now enrolled to do a Duke of Edinburgh's Gold Award.

5C
Access

The issue of physical accessibility to resources and services has long been recognised as a key factor affecting the quality of life in rural areas. Some of the benefits which adults believe young people might gain from living in a rural area tend to be nullified by the difficulties they face in getting access to the services they need that adults, especially those with their own transport, may underestimate.

On this basis many rural young people suffer from pronounced inequality of provision. They will need to invest time, energy and money in travelling to use the most basic services, which may still be of a more restricted type and poorer quality than those found in urban areas. At the same time they have little chance of encountering the range of specialist services for young people which are starting to emerge in urban areas, unless statutory and voluntary agencies have been able to mount special rural initiatives. This section documents some of the structural difficulties encountered by young people in trying to achieve their basic entitlements.

EDUCATION

The Issues

Many rural locations have lost their primary schools in recent years, losing a focal point for village life for children and parents alike. A number of factors can conspire to limit access to education:

- long distances to secondary schools reduces the choice of schools;
- problematic school bus schedules;
- little opportunity, without personal transport, to socialise after school;
- reduced parental involvement in school life;
- subjects, facilities and equipment may all be more restricted and of poorer quality;
- larger schools may reduce security and involvement;
- victims of bullying on the school bus will find it hard to take evasive action;
- difficulty in arranging alternative education for young people who are excluded from school; and
- seasonal truancy.

Youth Work Responses

Rural schools and the schools that are used by young people living in rural areas are important resources. Many are increasing their community role and offering access beyond normal school hours, with staff taking an increasingly proactive role in community affairs. Youth workers can capitalise on these trends by:

- use of school and school buses as contact points for young people in a given catchment area;
- use of school as a base for outreach work;
- offering input on issues not tackled easily within the normal school curriculum – cross curriculum themes, aspects of personal and social education;
- providing information and advice geared to personal need, and to address issues such as sexual health;
- working creatively with schools to influence wider provision;
- developing ways of supporting disaffected pupils and their parents;
- using the school as an information point for young people about non-school matters; and
- working with parents/parent teacher associations and governors.

Practice Examples

♦ In the East Midlands young people living in very isolated villages had no opportunity to communicate with each other outside of school hours. When bringing them together at a youth centre proved to be impractical, the youth worker initiated the idea of a newsletter which young people contributed to and published. This was initially organised at one of the schools during lunchtimes and contained news of local events in the area and comments on issues of interest to young people. With a circulation of 200, it provided a way of keeping in touch with isolated individuals and a mechanism for organising trips.

♦ Youth workers in the West Midlands developed a youth arts group for young people who were feeling frustrated at their inability to find a means of exploring their own creativity within an increasingly restrictive school curriculum. One full-time and two part-time youth workers with arts skills were able to offer a wide range of activities, including music, drama and a variety of visual arts.

Some of the group wanted to do some large scale painting using graffiti and spray techniques and a one-day workshop was organised at a youth centre with a practising artist from Liverpool invited to join them. The artist used a range of skills and techniques new to the young people which, together with the scale of the work, gave them a sense of freedom they had not experienced before. Inspired by this enthusiasm they organised a series of successful workshops of their own for other young people, demonstrating what they had learnt.

♦ A youth worker on the Welsh Borders found himself supporting quite a few young people who were sexually active but had little or no concept of the risks they were taking with unsafe sexual practices, as well as lacking maturity in their approaches to relationships and intimacy. Since he could only reach a small number of young people in this way he approached the local comprehensive school with the aim of offering his skills to complement the existing school-based sex education.

Sessions were arranged during registration and tutorial periods for young people from Year 11 to play *The Grapevine Game* in small peer groups with the possibility of a follow-up hour at lunchtime. Following the success of this the sessions have been opened up to young people in the fourth year who play other games of a similar nature such as *Time of the Month* or *Man's World*. Young people have the chance to discuss sexual matters in an informal environment and the youth worker has developed a network of health professionals to provide specialist information as required.

TRAINING/FURTHER EDUCATION/CAREERS

The Issues

Vocational training on offer in rural areas is frequently limited in choice and stereotypical in terms of the range of options available both for young men and young women. The travel needed to reach a suitable course or training place may be prohibitive or the preferred options just not available locally. Other issues include:

♦ possible inadequate information about FE and vocational courses;

♦ probable gap between available provision and needs of young people and the local labour market;

♦ need for potentially lengthy travel to major centres of population for study, training and careers advice – reducing capacity for training/study;

♦ possibility of rigid course structure with little flexibility, especially for women with young children, or other domestic/care responsibilities;

♦ proposals to privatise careers service (pilots are currently operating in a number of areas) may further limit access to rural young people;

♦ impossible travel logistics entailing a move to the town or city to take up place at college or training establishment, possibly without family or community support;

♦ lack of self-confidence, particularly among young women, preventing acceptance of a course of study or a training place which requires a major move away from home;

♦ difficulty in obtaining affordable accommodation in areas with high tourist and/or transient population if moving away from home to train or study;

♦ reduced alternatives if a place is lost or rejected for any reason;

♦ administrative regulations regarding funding or travel preventing acceptance of an appropriate training place in a neighbouring county which is closer than own county-based centre; and

♦ travel and other issues acting as deterrents to a particular scheme, making it difficult for it to retain its viability.

Youth Work Responses

Youth workers are better placed than most adults to:

♦ ensure that relevant information about study and training opportunities reaches young people who need it through outreach work, information access points and computerised resources;

♦ work with FE colleges and TECs to offer a youth work perspective on provision for young people and support for individuals;

♦ act as advocates for individuals or groups with special/equal opportunity needs; and

♦ work strategically with a range of agencies to improve overall provision.

Practice Examples

♦ A mobile bus organised by the youth and community service in a deep rural upland area has been supplied with computers from the local training centres to provide careers advice. Through interviews with young people and the use of low key questionnaires to identify their interests and ambitions, printouts can be given on training qualifications and available courses. In one short project ten villages were serviced over a five-day period.

♦ Youth workers in a Home Counties rural patch recognised the need to follow up guidance work started in school with young people in the rural areas of the county who were identified as demotivated and unlikely to benefit from traditional vocational courses. A combination of barriers was identified. These included lack of personal confidence, relationship problems within the family, poor experience of institutions, cost of course fees, lack of flexibility in courses, lack of guidance, lack of suitable accommodation, discrimination and negative attitudes from staff and other learners.

A pilot scheme was begun, funded by the local TEC with cooperation between the youth service, adult education guidance service, Department of Employment and the new local university, to look at how to improve access and take up.

A free, eight-week course was held, based at a youth centre, once a week from 10.00am – 3.00pm offering young people free transport, free lunch and the opportunity to sample different options. The project increased confidence, offered information on grants, individual guidance sessions, follow up and support, and participants were awarded a certificate from the university. Workshops were offered on computers and music technology, painting and decorating, community care and social work, basic motor mechanics, working with videos, setting up a business, photography and design and creative arts.

EMPLOYMENT

The Issues

Many rural areas have unemployment figures far above the national average (and the average for the region) creating pockets of severe hidden deprivation. Where jobs exist, choice is likely to be restricted and stereotypical. Other factors include:

♦ intermittent seasonal jobs (especially in agriculture and tourism) leading to under employment;

♦ high levels of self-employment;

♦ low pay, long hours, poor safety records in some sections and low levels of unionisation (the loss of the agricultural wages council is likely to further depress rural wages);

♦ predominance of informal, temporary employment;

♦ nepotism – many vacancies never reach the public domain;

♦ the difficulty of childcare outside of family networks;

♦ the reality that many young people may ultimately be forced to move to secure employment; and

♦ the fact that working locally may restrict opportunities to establish a separate identity away from family and community expectations.

Youth Work Responses

In work with older young people, rural workers need to be increasingly active and alert to employment issues. Youth workers can:

- ensure information and advice is made available to young people in their own locations;
- address issues of childcare provision to support young parents;
- consider inter-agency initiatives which can lead to job creation;
- help young people acquire marketable skills;
- gain access to influence local TECs;
- widen horizons for young people pre-16; and
- encourage local employers to make job vacancies more widely known.

Practice Example

♦ A recent initiative by the National Federation of Young Farmers' Clubs was to persuade the Ministry of Agriculture to deregulate access to land and farm buildings so that self-employment opportunities could be developed for young people who wanted to stay and work in their local communities. This would give them the chance to use skills such as craft work learnt in their local YFC club and develop their own business. The Federation has also reached agreement with a national bank for them to run a venture club award which would provide young people with professional and managerial advice on running their business and access to prize money and loans.

HEALTH CARE

The Issues

Confusion among many GPs about young people's rights to confidential treatment can mean numbers of young people in rural areas may not seek the health care they might need. Fears of information getting back to parents through close knit social networks can also inhibit take up. Other factors that can affect access to health care include:
- long periods before emergency care is received because of distances to hospital casualty departments and long journey times for ambulances;
- sensitivities of traditional exposed rural communities to overt discussion around sex education or damage limitation approaches to drugs education leading to lack of access to advice on contraception, sexual health, HIV and AIDS and drug misuse;
- HIV/AIDS sufferers likely to face lack of privacy and hostile attitudes with minimal support networks available; and
- need for travel in many cases outside village to obtain basic health care, with difficult public transport logistics.

Youth Work Responses

Many youth work projects already provide information and advice on health issues including alcohol, drugs, smoking and HIV/AIDS through curriculum/outreach work, taking account of the sensitivity of local rural communities. Other roles include:
- providing objective sex education and assistance with access to contraception advice;
- providing first aid courses and accident prevention awareness;
- developing inter-agency links so that issues can be addressed via existing youth work groupings in villages;
- taking advantage of national health promotion initiatives; and
- rehearsing action needed in case of emergency.

Practice Examples

♦ Local authority youth workers researched the needs of young women in a number of Home Counties villages and identified a need for them to meet on a regular basis to look at issues relevant to their sexuality. A programme of activities was organised, the project was publicised and transport to bring the young women to a central point arranged. As well as offering discussion, the programme enabled the young women involved to visit a keep fit facility and spend an evening at a sex education project looking at contraception and safe sex issues.

♦ A mobile in the East Midlands area, supported by the youth service, has recruited part-time workers locally to train in health and to specialise in health promotion with young people who are attracted to the mobile during its visits to villages. This increases scope for informal support and ensures the young people have a local point for information and advice as and when they need it.

♦ St John Ambulance runs youth groups throughout the country. A development worker in the Southwest provided specialist support to local volunteers running groups for young people in rural areas. These groups help young people gain greater knowledge of first aid, which may be very necessary when the nearest medical help may be many miles away. In addition, workers expand their social and personal education work with young people, particularly in areas where there might be few other types of youth provision.

♦ A project sponsored by a health authority in East Anglia provides four part-time workers to promote social education programmes on health issues. A major focus of the project is teenage pregnancy. Workers are trained and experienced health educators who work alongside rural youth workers in providing information, informal teaching and referrals about general health care.

SPORT/OUTDOOR ACTIVITIES/ENVIRONMENT

The Issues

Changing land use and lack of acknowledgment of needs means few play or activity opportunities for many young people in rural areas compared with their urban counterparts.

Specific examples include:
♦ few opportunities to take up a sport seriously because of the logistics of organising access to coaching and equipment;
♦ expensive access to sport and leisure opportunities in local towns which is time consuming and difficult because of lack of transport, especially in the evening;
♦ inequality of provision between rural and urban young people visible if supervised urban groups are using the countryside for organised, well-equipped recreation; and
♦ fewer opportunities for trips to different types of setting for rural youth groups than for many urban ones.

Youth Work Responses

Rural youth workers can make an important contribution to organising transport to ensure access to sport and leisure opportunities in the nearest urban centres. They can also:
♦ ensure equal access by groups, such as disabled young people;
♦ make inter-agency links to organise summer playschemes/activity weeks;
♦ organise trips to different types of rural location to widen experiences;
♦ make links with urban youth work groups using district colleagues for mutual exchange;
♦ work strategically with sport and leisure providers to ensure relevance of provision to young people's needs; and
♦ broaden young people's understanding of and involvement in environmental issues.

Practice Examples

♦ The Groundwork Trust is a national charity which contributes to environmental projects through partnership with industry, the private sector, local authorities and voluntary organisations. Individual projects vary but include making factory sites more environmentally-friendly, bringing new life to derelict land and restoring or opening up footpaths and bridleways. In 1990 a specialist youth worker was appointed to engage young people in environmental projects in former pit villages in a Northeastern industrial area. Such villages have declining services and very few youth facilities.

Groundwork, with resources of equipment, transport and ideas of things to do, has found itself increasingly in demand and developed a whole range of strategies with which to respond. The recruitment of a local volunteer helped with the harnessing of local people and resources. Initial contact with young people is targeted according to identifiable needs – for example, visible groups of uninvolved young people or requests from a parish council. Groups are then offered experiences and learning from a repertoire of possibilities including outdoor activities, conservation work and environmental projects.

The next phase is to help the group identify a task or activity for themselves – planting out a local site, clearing a local eyesore or trying to secure their own youth centre. The Groundwork project has visibly changed patterns of youth work with a number of local villages – parish councils now approach the project for ideas and advice and a number of areas of derelict land are being revitalised.

♦ A group of young women from a rural industrial area in the Midlands, with youth work support, organised a weekend in Cumbria with the aim of taking part in outdoor adventurous activities which would present them with new challenges and experiences. The weekend enabled the young people to participate in riding, climbing, caving, fell-walking, mountain biking, abseiling, dry-slope skiing and Canadian canoeing – experiences that were new to many of them and which increased confidence and led to some taking up new activities on a regular basis.

♦ The Rural Community Council in a Home Counties area contacted a local football club to follow up a 'football in the community scheme'

run by the major footballing organisations, which takes sport and coaching facilities out to people in rural areas – offering opportunities that they might not have had before. The Rural Community Council advertised the scheme in the rural parts of the county through village newsletters, youth clubs, the local press and the RCC magazine. Take-up from village clubs enabled access to a level of coaching previously out of reach of village communities.

♦ The National Federation of Young Farmers' Clubs ran an initiative in which every club in England and Wales took part in an environmental activity during one week in April 1992. Groups cleared churchyards and footpaths and one club in the Southwest created an amenity area from derelict land in partnership with a City Farm and an 18+ group.

HOUSING AND HOMELESSNESS

The Issues

Little rural housing is available to the indigenous population and that which exists is increasingly diverted to the more profitable incomer market. New housing developments in rural areas are not guaranteed to be geared to local needs unless they are part of an initiative by a housing association or local agency. Young people, therefore, are being progressively shut out from local housing options in rural areas because:

♦ they are ineligible for public housing at 16 and low priority on most waiting lists from 18;

♦ they are unable to compete with incomers for private housing because of price;

♦ much of the suitable rented sector property had been sold off for owner occupation, second homes or holiday lets with visitors taking priority;

♦ remaining options are either undesirable or hazardous – for example, mobile homes, sleeping rough, tents, sleeping in cars;

- public housing may be unsuited to needs and lack the degree of personal support which is necessary at early stages of a tenancy;
- any accommodation offered may not be affordable by young people because the combined rent and running costs may take up too great a proportion of their already low income or benefit;
- lack of access to independent accommodation puts greater pressure on parents to continue to provide support in what may be an overcrowded home, further affecting the privacy of younger children;
- young women or young couples with children face a number of unsatisfactory options if independent accommodation is not available – increasing pressure on family resources, emergency accommodation for mother and child separate from father, or children taken into care; and
- lack of a stable address creates problems in maintaining a job, claiming benefit or being contacted for training, work.

Youth Work Responses

A range of youth work responses is appropriate: preparation for leaving home; support during housing crisis; and involvement in pressing for appropriate local provision. Practical activities can include:

- provision of emergency support, advice and accommodation;
- development of tenant and landlord support schemes;
- advocacy on behalf of young people with housing departments, housing associations, housing benefit office;
- influencing tenancy arrangements;
- pressing for provision of suitable single person accommodation;
- researching/establishing evidence of need in the local area and publicising the results; and
- participating in and stimulating inter-agency mobilisation to identify the most relevant response to local need.

Practice Examples

- A detached worker based in a coastal resort first identified the need for accessible accommodation for young people in 1988. In 1991 joint work by an inter-agency group resulted in the offer of a house from the district council. An adjoining cottage became available at a later date. Funds were raised from a wide range of sources and local young people involved on the management committee. The project initially targeted young people aged between 16 and 21, but will work with young people up to 25. The project became operational in March 1993 and offers crash pad accommodation for a short-term period, an advice shop and counselling services on a drop-in basis and a training programme in skills for independent living.

- An inter-agency group, including the youth and community service, sought to address the needs of the young and homeless in a Home Counties area. Youth workers identified a need for daytime provision for unemployed and homeless young people and arranged for a purpose-built youth centre to be available exclusively for them one day a week. The curriculum is geared to countering the psychological effects of homelessness and includes discussion groups, sessions on political and social issues, confidence building and participation in the Duke of Edinburgh's Award. The project is funded jointly by the youth service and the probation service, with two workers providing support. Young people have participated in a range of activities, but their emerging self-confidence is best demonstrated by having run a workshop at a high-profile conference on housing and homelessness.

- A Southwest downland area identified a problem for young people obtaining accommodation in tourist areas. An inter-agency steering group including youth workers obtained funding to appoint an accommodation officer to set up a supported lodging scheme for young people. The youth service provided a free base in one of their offices.

♦ National initiatives on housing and homelessness have included leaving home education work by the Leaving Home Project and Youth Clubs UK.

Groups of young people in rural areas and their youth workers have been undertaking two surveys. The first explores the expectations of young people leaving home and the second examines the experiences of young people who have already left home. The second phase involved the same groups analysing educational resources relating to housing education and assessing whether they meet the needs of young people in rural areas. The young people involved have gained insights into the realities of leaving home that will help them when their turn comes.

INFORMATION AND ADVICE

The Issues

Lack of immediately accessible and objective information and advice is a major problem for adults and young people alike in rural areas. The nearest services are likely to be in the closest small town with a generalist part-time Citizen's Advice Bureau (CAB). For young people the difficulties are compounded by:

♦ lack of accessible specialist youth advice and counselling schemes; ·

♦ lack of anonymity in making use of advice sources whether in the local town or via a mobile;

♦ lack of access to free and informed legal advice; and

♦ difficulty in sustaining counselling relationships at the appropriate frequency because of access difficulties.

This lack of access to information and advice underpins all the other access issues by limiting options on training, health, jobs and housing.

Youth Work Responses

Across the country youth workers are increasingly involved in developing specialist youth information and counselling services in market towns with outreach to surrounding areas. These can:

♦ train youth workers on basic legal rights/key issues for young people and suggest where to get detailed advice and information;

♦ develop local information survivor guides with young people;

♦ examine ways of ensuring confidentiality and privacy for individual enquirers; and

♦ develop inter-agency links to ensure young people's access to accurate information and advice can be made through a variety of sources.

Practice Examples

♦ A market town in a northern upland area provides the base for a youth enquiry service which acts as a focal point for the surrounding rural area. Early on in the life of the project it became clear that to make a serious offer of information, advice and potential counselling to young people in the sparsely populated area meant taking provision to them. A purpose-built caravan parked in school playgrounds enables the youth workers to provide direct access to enquirers and to become involved in parts of the personal and social education curriculum.

Arrangements vary in detail across the range of schools in the district, but all welcome the project team for perhaps a two-week period before they move off to another site. Contacts with young people generate on average three hundred enquiries a month, with queries on everything from consumer rights to drug information, legal advice or help with housing. Spin-offs from the project have included the development of new housing resources for young people and sub-offices of the enquiry service based at other youth clubs. The project is now developing support and training for local adult volunteers and concentrating on the counselling side of the work.

♦ A mobile information and advice project in a Home Counties rural area offers a service to young people living in isolated rural areas through targeting specific villages for regular evening visits. The project offers specific information on housing and homelessness, and is equipped with a list of local accommodation. Information is also carried on welfare rights, health, vocational training and leisure facilities. Attempts to establish the needs and concerns of young people have been undertaken through questionnaires. An inter-agency group funds the project, including four workers each with six youth work sessions per week.

♦ As part of its outreach provision, a counselling centre in East Anglia provides a part-time worker for two sessions a week to work in youth centres in two rural market towns. Joint funded projects for the provision of a counselling room, payment of worker and advertising have been supported by the local town councils, charitable trusts and the RDC. Evidence so far suggests that the services are well used, and there are good cooperative links with local high schools, the youth service and other agencies.

6

Factors Affecting Future Delivery

6A
The Current Climate

During the life of the rural project at the NYA, youth work in all sectors has been challenged by changes going on both within the service and outside it. Across the country, there is scarcely a single youth service organisation that has not undergone review – finding itself having to raise its profile, become more accountable and in many situations do both with shrinking resources.

Within the voluntary sector, many national and local voluntary youth organisations have reasserted their identity or contemplated a change in the way they present their work to the public. For services in the public sector, fundamental questions about the roles and responsibilities of local authorities have placed the spotlight on each service in turn, such that county council youth services have been forced to declare their purpose and value more clearly. In response youth work organisations have produced a mass of new policy documents, curriculum packs, business plans, strategy documents and other statements of intent

designed to secure their organisation's place within the foreseeable future.

Much of this has been driven by the need for the youth service to find a more coherent identity that enables it to assert its place within the changing world of education. More desperately it also comes from a desire to survive at all at a time when consensus about the validity of social education has been fast evaporating.

Legislation

Some of the changes of the past three years have been precipitated directly by legislation, others more by sets of underlying trends that reinforce the need to demonstrate efficiency at delivering a service that the public (and by implication the Government) need to be told they would miss were it not there.

For many practitioners, the changes of the past few years have been experienced as change for change's sake – alterations to arrangements that have long proved their worth, seemingly for reasons of political dogma. Many workers express an uneasy sense that the pressures and changes have been aiming to destabilise rather than to improve. In truth, many of the changes affecting youth work have been because of the absence of attention to its role and purpose rather than a predetermined effort to dismantle it, so that youth work practice has been swept up in changes in which its existence had been scarcely noticed.

The most cogent example of this is the lack of any direct reference to the youth service within the legislation that is now transforming the delivery of further education. The 1992 Further and Higher Education Act has taken away from local authorities the responsibility for funding local vocational adult education (more or less everything that leads to qualifications/examinations) and requires individual colleges or local consortia to bid to a new national body, the Further Education Funding Council (FEFC), for its funds. Here the nearest statement to a validation of the youth service is contained in the reference to an authority's responsibility to: 'secure the provision for their area of adequate facilities for further education', and that further education means:

a) *full-time and part-time education suitable to the requirements of persons over compulsory school age (including vocational, social, physical and recreational training); and*

b) *organised leisure-time occupation provided in connection with the provision of such education.*

Lack of Recognition

This absence of explicit attention to the location, structure and role of youth services, so soon after the service had been directly challenged by a series of junior education ministers to describe precisely its unique contribution to young people's education, was a disappointment. This, combined with the trend towards Government support through short-term project funding, suggested to many that youth work is viewed as a convenient

afterthought that can be bought in at will to tackle flashpoint situations where groups of young people transgress publicly acceptable boundaries of behaviour. The low legislative profile is further illustrated by other legislation since 1989 that affects youth work but does not attempt to describe it nor secure its place. This includes:

♦ the series of Local Government Acts creating the 'enabling' authority, reducing direct delivery and extending the range of services required to be put to competitive tender;

♦ education legislation that first developed the local management of schools (LMS) (the 1988 Education Reform Act) then encouraged individual schools to become grant maintained and to sever links with local education authorities altogether (GMS);

♦ charity reforms placing new requirements on voluntary organisations; and

♦ new childcare legislation requiring local authorities to protect children and young people in need (the 1989 Children Act).

At the time of writing the latest Education Bill based on the white paper *Choice and Diversity – A New Framework for Schools* proposes further changes that remove the need for local authority education committees altogether and could lead to further loss of access to some premises originally built for youth work use.

Other Influences

In 1991 the DES-commissioned report on the management of the youth service (the Coopers and Lybrand Deloitte report) was formally published. The report studied arrangements across a range of local authorities including 23 rural shires. Its recommendations focused on the need for fundamental improvements to youth service management processes and recognised the importance of local delivery through a combination of sectors – validating the work of the maintained, voluntary and independent sectors alike and recognising the proportion of work now taking place outside the established voluntary sector and beyond mainstream local authority work.

The rapid contraction of local education authority school and FE administrations, together with the push in some authorities towards wholesale contracting out of services, drove home the need to reassess future possibilities. Suddenly everything was being reassessed at the same time – the location of the youth service within the local authority structure; the place and role of voluntary sector provision; and the basic shape of youth work on the ground. External forces, internal influences and shifts in the culture of many organisations therefore have been potent forces for change. So too is money.

Spending

The single factor that currently determines the ultimate extent of local authority support for youth work on the ground is each local authority's Standard Spending Assessment (SSA). Provision for youth work comes out of what is described as the 'other education' block – the level of funding within the overall SSA that Government believes each local authority should be spending on services that fall outside their statutory responsibilities – for example, residual FE provision, non-vocational adult education and the youth service.

Support for youth work from elected members has therefore become a critical factor in determining levels of resource allocation locally. Youth work can no longer take for granted its place in the priority of needs that a local authority has to address, and even where it is prioritised, the chances are that unless there is concerted effort to focus attention on rurality, urban needs will prevail.

Political Profile

Between the first youth service ministerial conference in 1989 and the second in 1990 many shire county youth services seized on the creation of the mission statement for the youth service nationally as an opportunity to raise their profile at the local level. Processes often involved elected members, young people, voluntary organisations and workers in the quest for a comprehensive statement that would describe and validate all youth work taking place within the geographical area of the local authority. This meant including the range of work taking place within the non-municipal sector, including the local branches of National Voluntary Youth Organisations (NVYOs) and those wholly local organisations and projects that deliver a substantial proportion of youth work in all rural areas.

Emerging Delivery Options

With all of this as its context, an early project within the newly-formed NYA during the 1991–92 year worked with a small number of youth service organisations as they developed responses to the new situations they would be facing during the 1991–92 year and beyond. This project – entitled Delivering Local Youth Services (DLYS) – is comprehensively written up in the publication *Facing Facts – the Future Delivery of Local Youth Services* published by the NYA in 1992 [61.2]. Invitations for involvement in the project went to all local authority and national voluntary sector youth organisations contemplating rapid change. In the event, five local authorities took part together with one voluntary sector consortium: three London boroughs – Bexley, Bromley and Croydon; two Midlands shire counties – Staffordshire and Warwickshire; and a consortium of voluntary providers in the Northeast under the umbrella of Youth Clubs UK.

The destinies that emerged for this handful of youth services over the course of just one year are an object lesson in the pace of change at that time. At the start of the project, Croydon was heading for delivery of its youth service via contracts with voluntary organisations and the commercial/private sector. Bromley and its outer London neighbour Bexley were heading for similar, if more measured, moves towards the introduction of contracting. Staffordshire was considering reorganisation into newly-defined areas, coupled with the delegation of budgets to area teams, and Warwickshire was considering a range of options.

By mid 1992 (less than a year), the agenda to sub-contract in Croydon was being rapidly reconsidered; Bromley was well on the way to shedding all its local authority employed full-time youth officers and workers, and Bexley was proceeding towards tendering but at a more modest pace.

In the shire counties involved, Warwickshire Youth Service was suddenly facing the dismantling of its previous structure and the retention of a team charged with the task of developing contracts with the voluntary sector. Only Staffordshire was on its original course of combining an internal restructuring with changes in budget arrangements. In each of these authorities relationships with the voluntary youth sector were crucially tested as various options emerged – the one wholly voluntary sector initiative designed to prepare for the prospects of bidding and contracts found itself operating within a region where contracting was developing at the slowest pace.

There was a clear north/south divide evident here with different responses to pressures for change. However, despite the variability of the immediate outcomes for the organisations concerned, a number of patterns were able to be distinguished which suggested a range of likely scenarios for the shape and characteristics for many other youth services in the near future. The delivery options identified by the DLYS project by the time of its completion in April 1992 were:

1   Securing a fully maintained service: acknowledging the diversity of local arrangements and the ability of some services to adapt to changing cultures without fundamentally altering either their shape or most practical arrangements.

2   Delegation: enabling decisions about on-the-ground delivery within a local authority service to be made at the lowest feasible level – achieved by allocating funds, perhaps using complex formulae, to local teams or districts while retaining some strategic functions at the centre.

3   Single line budgets: the youth service becoming an organisation in its own right with its managers exercising control over spending and perhaps reporting to a board of directors rather than a local authority committee. Funding to such a Direct Service Organisation was seen as likely to be by contract or service level agreement with the local authority. Staff would be expected to remain local authority employees.

4   Non-profitmaking trusts: newly-created companies (possibly with charitable status) with the majority of their funds coming from contracts with the local authority. The local authority would retain a controlling majority of seats on the board of the new company. Existing staff would probably become employees of the new company.

5   A company outside local authority control: organisations would manage their own resources and be able to raise their own capital and revenue. Companies might have contracts with a number of local authorities (and other funders). Staff would be employees of the company. Any seats on the board of management held by the local authority would be insufficient to exert control.

6   Open bidding for contracts: any number of organisations might be invited to tender against specifications for services drawn up by the local authority. Tenders might be invited from known organisations or by open advertisement.

It is important to remember that these were models only, which were not mutually exclusive. However, the sequence of these models was seen to represent a decreasing level of local authority control: in the first three, the local authority would retain direct responsibility for the work it funds, in models four and five responsibility for delivery would be with organisations outside its direct control. For model six the authority's influence could be exerted only through the drawing up of its expectations in the form of a contract specification and subsequent monitoring of the work to that framework.

The Contract Culture

As models these six options were designed to illustrate the consequences of the expected move towards substantial degrees of contracting – ensuring youth service managers were alert to the implications and able to make informed choices about how to respond if such shifts were being proposed locally.

Writing a further year on, the number of shire authorities that have openly moved towards some of the more radical options are few. However, what is evident is that the contract culture has become a powerful feature of local authority work with whole departments now experiencing moves toward privatisation, including many services not so far away from the youth service in terms of both philosophy and client groups – social service departments and careers services being obvious examples.

What is also apparent is that increasingly, discrete elements of youth service provision are being set up to be operated as separate cost-centres – for example, residential centres – having to balance their own budgets by marketing themselves beyond the youth service. Other clear trends include the creation of specialist projects invited to bid for development grants.

6B
The Consequences For Rural Work

Together, these developments have consequences for work in rural areas by the local authority maintained sector and for the traditional voluntary sector providers/independent sector alike. How the needs of young people in rural areas are presented to local authorities is an increasingly important factor in securing resources. This is going to be the case almost regardless of local arrangements for budget allocation, receiving bids for funding. Workers and managers in rural areas must ensure that in the scramble for change or in the rush to respond to it, the needs of the young people they work with (or wish to work with) are made explicit. It is important, therefore, to explore both the benefits and the disadvantages of these kinds of options and to look carefully and imaginatively for opportunities that might secure a better deal for the young people concerned.

One of the most significant opportunities is the scope increasing use of contracts gives voluntary and independent sector organisations to increase their influence. Both national and local organisations might be well placed to operate either existing provision or to develop new projects in rural areas, tailoring the work to identifiable local needs and developing new and exciting approaches in the process. On the other hand the regimes are likely to be tougher; contracts will probably be subject to stricter accountability through monitoring arrangements. The impact of monitoring regimes, unless sensitively negotiated with workers at all levels, ensuring everyone understands the need for and significance of recording data, can lead to diversion from the real task and demotivation of those in direct contact with young people.

There are also other risks: the potential fragmentation of services across larger geographical areas, the difficulty for voluntary organisations of dealing with more sponsoring organisations and the importance within any contractual system of getting the terms of the agreement right in the first place – setting out clear expectations on both sides and then ensuring that what is promised is delivered in practice.

Local Authority Structures and Boundaries

The next factor taxing many rural youth service organisations concerns the prospects of redrawn county and district boundaries as a result of the work of the Local Government Commission. The Commission's brief is to review '… (the) present structures and boundaries of (English) county and district councils'. The stated intention is to end public confusion over roles, to improve coordination in service delivery and to reduce bureaucracy.

Creating the Commission was part of the 1992 Local Government Act. Earlier legislation had already reduced the local authority's role as a direct provider of services and required the extension of compulsory competitive tendering to white collar functions.

For youth work in general and work in rural areas in particular the location of the youth service in any future local authority departmental structure is a major concern. The vast majority of youth services are in education. However, they can be successfully located elsewhere. Nottinghamshire, for example, a county with significant rural areas, has shown itself able to develop high quality youth provision (and to protect it) while locating youth work within the Leisure Services Department. Other metropolitan authorities which include rural and sub-rural areas within their borders have also demonstrated the ability of predominantly urban authorities to provide services to rural youth from within a leisure services department.

Evidence of the interest of district councils in responding to the needs of youth service age ranges began to appear in a coherent form late in 1992. Up until the publication by the Association of District Councils of a paper entitled *Towards Unitary Authorities – Youth Service* in 1992, interest from and involvement in youth provision by districts was distinctly limited. With some notable exceptions, especially in the Southwest, few district councils are known to contribute financially to youth work. From the other perspective though, there has been little evidence in the past of county council youth services engaging with districts in any systematic and meaningful way. The prospects of enforced change as a result of local government reorganisation, however, are rapidly reframing people's thinking. New relationships are being explored and a new mutuality being forged, borne out of necessity.

For young people in rural areas this is good news. District (and parish/town) councils, which are beginning to believe that it is beneficial to invest in the young people whose life chances are bound up with the fortunes of the local area, offer the prospect of a new dimension to work with young people in rural areas. The changes that take place in the first new authorities are going to be interesting to watch. On the evidence so far, the likely size and shape of most of the new authorities is going to be somewhere between the smaller existing counties and the larger current districts. Some of these new authorities look likely to be substantially more rural than their predecessors. While youth work provision will have been one of the last factors to influence the Commission's thinking, the scale of the new councils and their greater demographic coherence may well enhance the possibilities of delivering a package of provision more clearly matched to the needs of young people who live in those rural areas.

The implications of the anticipated changes should be fully explored, looking at the scope to introduce coherent youth policies and to place services to youth on the 'high table' of the new authorities. New relationships will also be possible both with and between voluntary sector providers, and there is an opportunity within the process for young people to find a more powerful voice in the proceedings.

Within whatever new local structures emerge, the education role is going to be less extensive than previously because of the parallel changes that have taken out most (vocational) adult education responsibilities at a stroke and that means losing schools to GMS status (in some counties one by one, in others en masse). Proportionately, therefore, youth services become a bigger player in education – no longer the 1 per cent marginal aspect of provision but suddenly essential to the survival of an education department. In areas where the youth service is already outside education the situation will be slightly different but with no less opportunities to find a new and higher profile.

The Drive for Quality

Wherever youth services are to be located in local government in the future and/or whatever their status as voluntary organisations, youth workers will continue their ceaseless drive for quality and effectiveness. The language of performance indicators, planning tools and evaluation techniques is now familiar to managers in all sectors as they find themselves more and more tied to funding that requires the submission of forward work programmes, business plans and the setting out of anticipated outcomes.

For workers who have not yet been exposed to the concepts or are not yet experienced in their application, the use of terms such as performance indicators or business plans can be oppressive and disempowering. However, systems that build on what is already understood, on recording progress towards objectives that enable workers to meaningfully reflect on their interventions *are* beneficial and can be used to enhance the quality of work. Quality controls do not have to be remote nor accountability imposed from elsewhere. As adults taking on the responsibility of working with young people, youth workers should be prepared to be accountable to the young people they work with and to the organisations in whose names

they act. The art is to find mechanisms that illustrate the quality and effectiveness of what is undertaken without undermining the workers' capacity to be responsive and person centred.

The current and almost universal application of outcome-led funding and performance reviews by Government departments and the increasing expectations of other funders – trusts, corporate funders and the whole not-for-profit sector – may have serious consequences for any work involving long lead times and relatively invisible change.

Work with young people in rural areas has both those features – the *time* needed to negotiate and establish provision, to gain credibility and to begin to effect change, and *invisibility* because of distance, scale and the focus of much work on individual attitudes and confidence. At present short-termism is rife. Most new money being introduced into youth work nationally is urban in focus, expected to demonstrate measurable results within short time scales and designed to tackle single topics. The work can become piecemeal.

It is unlikely that rural work will suddenly become the issue of the day for Government departments. What becomes all the more important, therefore, is securing the support of other local funders – charitable trusts, companies, TECs, and looking to Europe and beyond. The opportunity created by the formation of new authorities, however, gives real scope to establish fresh regimes and styles of work that retain the best of the old and apply the most useful of the new.

6C
Future Funding

The future funding of rural work is clearly critical. The difficulty of legitimising specialist rural work has limited resources and determined the shape of work to date. This still presents the greatest barrier to development. There are no instant sources of more funding nor easy answers for how to present a convincing case that begins to address the current imbalance of funding between urban and rural areas. However, securing funding for rural work at the expense of other needs and settings should not be the goal. Finding ways to liberate funding and resources from all manner of different organisations has long been part of the art of working with young people.

In the conclusions that follow we pull together some of the ways in which recent successful projects have been able to capitalise on the clear presentation of the needs of young people in rural areas to secure resources through a combination of coherent policies, comprehensive planning and effective partnerships.

7

Conclusions

Young people who find themselves living in rural areas have fundamentally the same needs as young people living anywhere else. It is the variability of access to provision to meet those needs that creates disadvantage. Currently the situation and longer term prospects of young people growing up in rural areas are shaped by a number of key factors:

♦ economic pressures and cultural values that can exert a powerful brake on personal aspirations and likely achievements;

♦ poor access to public services such as health care and basic amenities such as shops and ordinary leisure and social pursuits;

♦ poor access to organisations and services central to making the transition to adulthood – a limited range of educational options, poor access to careers advice and limited choice of vocational training; and

♦ limited or non-existent availability of specialist services for groups such as young parents, young people with disabilities, gay and lesbian young people and for more general information and advice.

Some of these, of course, are issues for young people everywhere, some also apply to adults living in rural areas. But for young

people the realities of rural living can lead to specific disadvantage caused through a combination of factors:

♦ distance – both practical and psychological;

♦ prevailing attitudes towards young people from adults;

♦ stereotyping by family history, gender, class;

♦ poor job prospects combined with low pay;

♦ little likelihood of access to affordable local housing;

♦ lack of economic independence; and

♦ legal age barriers – for example, to health advice, driving, and to social provision such as pubs.

The experiences for individual young people, therefore, may lead to degrees of disadvantage that are profound in their effect yet hidden from immediate view, making them all the harder to legitimise and consequently much more difficult to overcome.

There is consistent evidence from rural areas that this multi-layered disadvantage can equally affect young people who have lived in rural communities all their lives and incomers. The evidence is that these experiences and factors can lead to:

♦ lack of self-confidence;

- limited horizons;
- lack of motivation;
- unrealised potential;
- undermined capacity to make and sustain relationships;
- frustrated ambition; and
- poorly established personal identity.

Many young people in urban areas also find themselves confined to neighbourhoods and trapped within circumstances that limit their growth and potential. The difference for young people in rural areas lies not in the extent of the deprivation but with the reality that the evidence of unrealised potential among young people is already recognised in urban areas whereas it often remains hidden in rural settings. Urban disadvantage and poverty are a recognised phenomenon for which the arguments are well rehearsed. Urban concerns attract Government intervention, a range of responses from statutory authorities and sustain a complex web of voluntary sector organisations in both the established and independent sectors. The argument, therefore, is not to seek to divert funding from urban work but to release other resources for work in rural areas.

The need is to overcome the way in which rural deprivation and disadvantage have been systematically obscured by the idealisation of rural life. Its denial continues to be sustained by a powerful combination of vested interests from within established communities of rural dwellers and by the aspirations of incomers who wish to preserve notions of rural tranquillity.

Youth work organisations from all sectors ought to be in the vanguard of those attempting to address these issues. Some indeed have risen to the challenge with a range of imaginative youth work responses. The current rural youth work scene provides evidence of much good practice which can stand comparison with the best of urban youth work.

In some situations, however, youth work responses to the needs of young people in rural areas have remained muted – noticeable more by their absence than for their effect. In part this is a consequence of a range of factors both historical and contemporary that include:

- the origins of youth work as a response to urban deprivation and the continued importance of addressing urban issues;
- a widespread failure to recognise the extent and significance of rural deprivation both generally and in connection with young people;
- economies of scale requiring nearly all sectors and services to concentrate resources in centres of population;
- youth work responses invariably geared to the most numerous and vocal demands;
- Government-sponsored initiatives – Urban Programme, Safer Cities, City Challenge, Education Support Grants, invariably focused on urban concerns; and
- financial pressures on services, and for some rural areas significant recent reductions to the work of the maintained sector.

This long-standing lack of attention to rural areas leads to a current scenario where:

- many young people in rural areas are left without access to provision that is adequate for their basic social and leisure needs;
- there is limited access to social education opportunities that challenge some of the oppressions of individual rural lives; and
- local volunteers sometimes struggle to provide basic provision for young people often without either the resources, the personal support or the stimulation of new ideas to enable them to do the job effectively.

Even where recent initiatives have been designed to increase the extent of rural work, a number of fundamental weaknesses and/or flaws can still remain:

- single specialist rural youth work posts are covering large geographical areas, carrying heavy workloads with few resources, limited back-up and weak support arrangements;
- uncoordinated local initiatives are evident in all sectors – within maintained services, by the established voluntary sector and by wholly local initiatives;

- competition exists for local resources or between organisations for volunteers from within the local community creating division and waste;
- the frequent emphasis on basic leisure provision rather than targeted work undermines some of the potential benefits;
- initiatives are often being 'parachuted' in without local ownership for the work;
- expectations are being raised which cannot ultimately be met; and
- the scale of interventions is often too low.

Pressures on services will be great and the low priority given to rural work may not necessarily be conscious. But the real and legitimate needs of young people in rural areas cannot be met in a piecemeal fashion. Detailed attention to both planning and delivery is vital. The recommendations that follow identify key elements for consideration in establishing a fully-integrated response to the needs of young people in rural areas using a framework of:

1 recognition of the right to equal opportunities and entitlement
2 the need for clear policies
3 the need for strategic planning
4 partnership in funding and delivery
5 the need for systematic support and training
6 attention to aspects of curriculum and programme.

1
Entitlement

Over the past decade, the majority of youth work organisations have acknowledged that race, gender, sexual orientation, class and disability are fundamental to the lives of the young people they work with. Most have, therefore, ensured that both their policies and their practice are informed and influenced by those realities.

It is now time to add rurality to the list of factors that have a far-reaching effect on the

lives of the young people concerned. Rurality affects life chances. Youth work, can address the potential narrowness of the rural experience. A starting point for action could be a recognition of five basic premises:

1 young people living in rural areas are likely to experience specific marginalisation;
2 young people in rural areas have the same basic entitlement as their peers in urban areas to a youth work curriculum that is relevant, challenging, progressive and fully accessible;
3 an anti-discriminatory framework is as vital in rural areas as in urban settings where the realities of discrimination and prejudice are often more immediately visible;
4 youth work in rural areas developed as part of the mainstream of youth work practice – planned, coordinated, resourced and supported in such a way that an adequate standard of provision can be achieved; and
5 work with young people in rural areas has a distinctive approach – and is planned to engage with the particular needs identified. While models are of course transferable and will undoubtedly inform work elsewhere the appropriateness and replicability of particular styles of work, such as club-based work or the use of innovations such as mobiles, cannot be assumed.

2
Clear Policies

These principles can be included in policies which set out for each relevant service or organisation its commitment to ensuring specific curriculum entitlements are delivered. Statutory and voluntary organisations alike can look to a number of sources for endorsement of the legitimacy of rural work. Those contained in the Thompson Report ([90]) and the NACYS report *Youth Work in Rural Areas* ([56]) make a good starting point.

The existing policies of many national voluntary youth organisations include work in rural areas. The Scout Association and the Duke of Edinburgh's Award scheme, for example, have both mounted initiatives to ensure parity of access to their opportunities for young people in rural areas. All youth service organisations can take stock of their policies in relation to rural work.

♦ Some national voluntary youth organisations might need to examine closely how far their policies address rural deprivation and inequality.

♦ Rural work in all sectors may well benefit from being specifically identified, acknowledged and nurtured instead of being perceived as 'routine'.

♦ Local Councils for Voluntary Youth Service could take the initiative to focus the policies of the voluntary sector, influence the local authority at county level and engage with parishes and districts to encourage policy and practice development in anticipation of local government reorganisation.

♦ Local authority youth services could examine not just their youth service policies but how far other policy statements concerning services to people in sparsely populated areas contain helpful references or statements and help to integrate service provision.

♦ Work may well need to be done beyond the immediate orbit of the youth service – especially to influence other sectors and organisations to think more clearly about the needs of young people as a legitimate part of their constituency.

♦ Recognition is needed that policies alone neither determine or guarantee the quality or effectiveness of practice on the ground.

3
Strategic Planning

In order to ensure coherence for young people in rural areas and to maximise the resources available, the growth of inter-departmental strategy groups can be a significant development. Charged with examining the needs of young people living in those rural areas they can also determine and implement policy. The key tasks of such a group could include determining needs, identifying priorities and securing resources. A more detailed remit might include:

♦ agreeing a common purpose for work with young people in the rural areas of the authority that can be expressed in policies and enacted in practice;

♦ commissioning research into local area needs;

♦ determining priorities for action in response to identified need;

♦ allocating resources and securing a long-term funding strategy;

♦ commissioning, coordinating and monitoring delivery;

♦ ensuring appropriate responses to changing needs and circumstances; and

♦ ensuring the provision of appropriate training.

Membership would hopefully include senior officers and members from a range of local authority services and appropriate voluntary sector providers and coordinating bodies as well as TECs, Rural Community Councils and the private sector.

This structure can of course apply regardless of the outcome of the current local government review and probably needs to be replicated at an operation level where membership could include local schools, local practitioners and other individuals and bodies having a legitimate contribution. Tasks here could then include:

♦ auditing existing resources;

♦ harnessing local community support including existing and potential local funding, voluntary effort and management skills;

♦ responsibility for local implementation of overall policies;

♦ planning, coordinating and monitoring local projects and initiatives;

- provision of local training and support; and
- recognition of the complexities and demands of managing youth work.

4
Partnerships

Significant opportunities for young people in rural areas will only be opened if resources are harnessed at a scale and for periods of time that enable viable projects and developments to take place. Too many initiatives to date have been either too small in number or too short in duration to make a difference.

Work with young people in rural areas is less likely to develop with reliance on a single source of funding whether from voluntary organisations, trusts, businesses, from Government sources or from local authorities. Young people's needs span the responsibilities of a number of local authority services and the potential interests of a range of voluntary organisations and non-departmental Government bodies and this can be used to advantage.

Improving services on the ground will require a practical commitment to partnership – sector to sector, organisation to organisation and between service providers. For partnerships to work, needs have to be met on all sides and at all levels. Joint work requires joint planning, shared strategies, agreed values and partnerships manifest at all levels – from executive to volunteer. And they need to address everything from bids for funding through to implementation and review.

Such partnerships may be difficult to achieve but they are possible. In practice, they require individual organisations and services to look beyond their usual role, reduce their competitiveness and focus on working for the advantage of the target group – focusing on the needs of young people in rural areas. This can be done by:

- creating new alliances between existing youth service organisations, particularly within the voluntary sector;
- creating new partnerships between youth work organisations and other services and sectors whose work impacts on (or has the potential to affect) young people living in rural areas;
- developing an agreed commitment to support the individual organisation or service best placed to operate in any given rural location – for example, encouraging movement beyond traditional organisational roles, labels and specialisms;
- recognising the value (the cost-equivalent) of voluntary effort and contributions in kind;
- acknowledging the entitlement of all stakeholders to test proposals being made and for organisations to examine each others work critically;
- avoiding competitive and 'hostile' bids for external funding by agreeing to a 'joint bids only' principle; and
- ensuring a commitment to realistic levels of funding for new projects and for a balance between core and programme funds.

5
Support and Training

Training is a critical issue for the development of more effective rural work and may need to be addressed at a range of levels. Frontline workers and volunteers need appropriate support at management and local level in order to effectively deal with the issues young people present and to help them overcome some of their own isolation. This may require action at a number of levels simultaneously:

- attention to the initial recruitment and ongoing support of local workers and volunteers;
- recognition of a likely resistance to training

by people who want to give their time directly to young people;

♦ the need to capitalise on offers of involvement from adults by not making the task too complicated yet encouraging awareness raising on issues such as gender stereotyping, the roots of prejudice and discrimination;

♦ offering skills training in particular youth work techniques such as outreach work, advocacy, information and advice work, crisis work, risk sports, outdoor activities;

♦ attention to the accessibility of support and training to voluntary workers, to senior members and to other young people wanting to get involved in the work;

♦ attention to harnessing the support of key players in rural communities – parish councillors, landowners, publicans, women's groups;

♦ encouragement of networking as a means of exchanging experiences and ideas;

♦ explicit support and supervision arrangements for workers at all levels; and

♦ the possible creation of centres of excellence where particular attention is paid to the evaluation of the work and to the recording and sharing of experiences via reports and training events.

6
Curriculum Delivery

Responding to the needs of young people in rural areas requires imagination, tenacity and clarity of task. Resources are likely to continue to be scarce which makes it all the more important that needs are accurately researched, priorities made, efforts targeted and appropriate offers made to the young people concerned. A number of principles can be applied:

♦ work at the unit level needs to be explicitly planned to address identified needs, issues, entitlements and to take account of other provision;

♦ practice needs to correlate with the principles and aims that have been developed in policies (and vice versa);

♦ workers need to know they are acting with the explicit support of their managers;

♦ work on issues should start where young people are and engage with young people's observations, actions, concerns and ideas;

♦ curriculum planning needs to leave space for immediacy;

♦ workers need to be alert to opportunities that allow for the exploration of specific themes as and when they arise;

♦ short-term goals need to relate to long-term strategies – avoiding short-term 'bandwagons';

♦ a range of approaches, activities and mediums needs to be in use that can be 'tested' for relevance against the needs that have been identified (balancing innovation and experience);

♦ high usage of curriculum materials needs to be evident;

♦ work and activities should be explicitly 'owned' by the young people involved and by the wider community;

♦ high levels of participation need to be sought and achieved;

♦ practical mechanisms need to be in place to evaluate the work; and

♦ work needs to be seen to be evaluated and learning applied to future actions.

Applied together these six principles lay the foundation for increasingly secure and effective practice in work with young people in rural areas. The listing does not claim to be exhaustive but offers a framework designed to maximise available resources, bring together a range of providers at local level, promote cooperation between organisations rather than competition and ensure that future provision for young people in rural areas is as coherent, meaningful and accessible as possible.

Appendix 1

Bibliography

Loan copies of these books and reports are available from the National Youth Agency Information Centre. Articles can be photocopied.

1   Archbishops' Commission on Rural Areas, **Faith in the Countryside**, Churchman Publishing, 1990

2   Akehurst, Michael et al, **Fieldwork: An aid to the support of youth workers**, National Association of Youth Clubs, 1984

3   Akehurst, Michael D., **Groundwork: Young people and the youth service in the countryside**, National Association of Youth Clubs, 1983

4   Akehurst, Michael and Marsland, David, **Victims of Myth: The situation of rural youth in Britain**, Akehurst and Marsland, 1981

5   Akehurst, Michael, **'Losers on the Rural Battlefield'**, *Youth in Society*, no. 49, December 1980, pp8-10

6   Akehurst, Michael, **Until the Fire and the Rose are One**, National Association of Youth Clubs, 1980

7   Albemarle, Diana Cicely Keppel, Countess of, **The Youth Service in England and Wales: Report of the committee**, HMSO, 1960

8   Ashley, Doreen, **Bus Shelters and Benches: A study of rural youth work in the Andover area**, Hampshire County Youth Service, 1991

9   Ball, Peter, **Rural Realities Rural Youth Work Research Project: Youth work in the Vale**, Oxfordshire County Council Community Education Vale Division, 1993

10 Barnes, Liz, **Getting Closer to Rural Communities: A rural resource paper giving some rural definitions**, National Council for Voluntary Organisations, 1993

11 Bonnar, Rosi, **Going Mobile: An introduction to the practicalities of working on a mobile community resource**, Mobile Projects Association, 1987

12 Burke, Tim, **'Travelling Light'**, *Young People Now*, no. 26, June 1991, p39

13 Button, Eleanor, **Rural Housing for Youth: A report on the causes and responses to youth homelessness in rural areas**, Centrepoint Soho, 1992

14 Campaign for Rural Youth, **Missed the Bus: A paper prepared by the campaign for rural youth for presentation to the youth parliamentary lobby**, Campaign for Rural Youth, 1979

15 Clark, Edith M., **Youth and the Village Club**, Thomas Nelson and Sons Ltd, 1946

16 Clark, John and Thornton, Wendy, **Keeping Them Off the Fields? A report on the establishing of a rural youth clubs association in north Lancashire**, Lancashire Youth Service, 1985

17 Community Development Department, **Planning and Managing a Scoutreach Project**, Scout Association, 1992

18 Corben, Jim, **Report on the National Symposium on Rural Youth Work held at Green Park Training Centre, Aston Clinton, Buckinghamshire, 10–12 September 1985**, National Youth Bureau, 1985

19 Costigan, Shirley, **We're on the Road: A report on the progress of the Teesdale Community Bus**, Teesdale Youth and Community Service, 1988

20 Cumbrian Association of Youth Clubs, **Report**, Cumbrian Association of Youth Clubs, 1992

21 Davies, Ron, **The Straight Banana: A further report on the Sandbach Area Mobile Youth and Community Unit**, Sandbach and Alsager Methodist Youth and Community Unit, 1990

22 Derbyshire County Council Youth Service, **Implementing the County Youth Service Policy in Rural Areas**, Derbyshire County Council Youth Service, 1989

23 Derounian, James Garo, **Another Country: Real life beyond rose cottage**, National Council for Voluntary Organisations, 1993

24 Devon Youth Service, **Reshaping the Youth Service**, Devon Youth Service, 1988

25 Duke of Edinburgh's Award, **The Duke of Edinburgh's Award Scheme in Rural Areas: Submission to the Duke of Edinburgh's Award's Special Projects Committee**, Duke of Edinburgh's Award, 1988

26 Duke of Edinburgh's Award, **Special Project: Inner city and rural initiatives**, Duke of Edinburgh's Award, 1990

27 East Hants Further Education Institute, **Rural Youth Work and the Youth Service in East Hants**, East Hants Further Education Institute, 1984

28 Eastleigh Mobile Youth Work Team, **Eastleigh Mobile Youth Work Team Annual Report June 1988–89**, Eastleigh Mobile Youth Work Team, 1989

29 Edmonds, K., **The Rea Hamlet Hopper: Taking the youth service to young people in rural Shropshire**, Shropshire Youth Service, 1992

30 Edwards-Rees, Désirée, **A Rural Youth Service: Suggestions for youth work in the countryside**, Religious Education Press Ltd, 1944

31 Fabes, Ray and Banks, Sarah, **'Working with Young People in Rural Areas'**, *Youth and Policy*, no. 33, May 1991, pp1–9

32 Fabes, Ray and Knowles, Cherie, **Working with Young People in Rural Areas**, Youth and Community Section: Leicester Polytechnic Occasional Paper, Leicester Polytechnic, 1991

33 Fabes, Ray and Popham, David, **Rural Mobiles**, National Youth Agency, 1993

34 See reference 55

35 Fussell, Michelle, **Rural Youth Work Project Report Pilot Year September 1992 to August 1993**, Berkshire Churches Project, 1993

36 Gelder, John, **Planning and Managing a Scoutreach Project**, Scout Association, 1991

37 Gelder, John, **Scoutreach in Rural Communities**, Community Development Department, Scout Association, 1991

38 Hampshire Youth Service, **Working with Young People in Rural Areas**, Hampshire Youth Service, 1993

39 Hertfordshire Youth and Community Service, **Policy for Rural Youth Work**, Hertfordshire County Council Education Department Youth and Community Service, 1989

40 Hindley, Ann, **Welcome All Children: Play and leisure opportunities of children with physical disabilities and learning difficulties living in rural Humberside**, Community Council of Humberside, 1992

41 Hogan, Jacqui, **'Building Bridges?'**, *Youth Clubs*, no. 55, November 1989, pp54–55

42 Humberside Youth Service, **Rural Strategy** (draft), Humberside Youth Service, 1993

43 Jay, Eric, **Keep Them in Birmingham: Challenging racism in southwest England**, Commission for Racial Equality, 1992

44 Johnson, Ian, **'Rural Life: A hope for young people?'**, *Youth and Policy*, no. 17, Summer 1986, pp9–12,

45 Kennedy, Allan, **Shadows of Adolescence: Images from west Dorset**, National Youth Bureau, 1984

46 Laflin, Clare, **Stepping Forward: A kit to enable rural churches to take positive steps towards meeting young people's needs**, United Reformed Church, 1987

47 Lambert, Christine et al, **Homelessness in Rural Areas**, Rural Development Commission, 1992

48 Lancashire Youth Service, **The Curriculum Development Group Report on Rural Youth Work**, Lancashire County Council, 1986

49 Leaving Home Project, LHP's Rural Research Project Update, **Leaving Home**, no. 11, May 1993, p4

50 Leicestershire Council for Voluntary Youth Services, **Bus Stops** (video), Leicestershire Council for Voluntary Youth Services, 1993

51 Lewis, Maureen, **A Time to Reflect: Report of a research project commissioned by Vale Girls and Young Women's Project**, Oxfordshire County Council Education Service, 1992

52 Lincolnshire County Council Youth Service and Lincolnshire Council for Voluntary Youth Services, **Lincolnshire Rural Youth Work Conference**, Lincolnshire Youth Service and Lincolnshire CVYS, 1990

53 MacDonald, Robert, **'Youth, Class and Locality in Rural England'**, *Youth and Policy*, no. 33, May 1991, pp17–26

54 Methodist Division of Education and Youth, **Young Ideas: A resource pack about rural churches and the under twenty–fives**, Methodist Division of Education and Youth and Methodist Home Mission Division, 1986

55 Milson, Fred W., and Fairbairn, Andrew N., **Youth and Community Work in the '70s: Proposals by the Youth Service Development Council**, HMSO, 1969

56 National Advisory Council for the Youth Service, **Youth Work in Rural Areas**, Department of Education and Science/Welsh Office, 1988

57 National Association of Youth and Community Education Officers, **Policy Statement Youth Work in Rural Areas**, NAYCEO, 1990

58 National Association of Youth Clubs, **Delivering Rural Youth Work**, National Association of Youth Clubs, 1984

59 National Children's Play and Recreation Unit, **Children Today in Devon: Playing in the countryside – a study of rural children's services**, National Children's Play and Recreation Unit, 1992

60 National Federation of Young Farmers' Clubs, **The YFC's Role in the 1990s**, National Federation of Young Farmers' Clubs

61 National Youth Agency, **Planning and Evaluation in a Time of Change: Report of the Third Ministerial Conference for the Youth Service**, National Youth Agency, 1992

61.1 National Youth Agency, **Working with Wheels Conference Report**, National Youth Agency, 1992

61.2 National Youth Agency, **Facing Facts – the future delivery of local youth services**, National Youth Agency, 1992

62 National Youth Agency, **Rural Youth Work Training Pack**, National Youth Agency, 1994

63 National Youth Bureau, **Report of the Second Symposium on Rural Youth Work held at Borwick Hall, Lancashire on 22–24 September 1986**, National Youth Bureau, 1986

64 National Youth Bureau, **Towards a Core Curriculum – The Next Step: Report of the Second Ministerial Conference**, National Youth Bureau, 1991

65 Newby, Howard, **Green and Pleasant Land?: Social change in rural England**, Hutchinson and Co (Publishers) Ltd, 1979

66 Northamptonshire Youth Service, **Northamptonshire Social Services, Interlink Bus: A multi-agency project**, Northamptonshire Youth Service, 1992

67 Nottinghamshire County Council, **Working with Travellers in Nottinghamshire**, Nottinghamshire County Council, 1993

68 Nottinghamshire Youth Service, **Rural Youth Work: Regional training conference report**, Nottinghamshire Youth Service, 1989

69 Opportunities Through Leisure Community Youth Association, **Hop on the Bus Community Youth Project**, Opportunities Through Leisure Community Youth Association, 1989

70 Popham, David, **Waterway Wanderings: Narrowboat residentials with young people from rural areas**, Churches Outreach Project, 1993

71 Popham, David and Susan, **Churches Outreach Project Annual Report 1992/93**, Churches Outreach Project, 1993

72 Regional Youth and Community Development Unit, **Northern Rural Youth Work Weekend 14–16 September 1990 at Beamish Hall, County Durham**, Regional Youth and Community Development Unit, 1991

73 Richards, Graham, **Rural Frontiers: A short study into the issues facing rural areas and their young people today**, Frontier Youth Trust, 1987

74 Rogers, Alan, **'Out of the Woods'**, *Youth Clubs with the Edge*, no. 66, February 1992, pp19–21

75 Rogers, Alan, **'The Inside Story'**, *Youth Clubs with the Edge*, no. 67, April 1992, pp26–29

76 Rural Development Commission, **Facts and Figures 1993/94**, Rural Development Commission, 1993

77 Rural Working Party, **County Rural Youth Work**, Buckinghamshire County Council, 1992

78 Rural Youth Work Working Group, **Identification of Good Practice in Rural Youth Work**, Lancashire Education Authority County Youth Service, 1987

79 S. Martin's College, **South Cumbrian Research Project for Hearing Impaired Young People**, S. Martin's College, 1991

80 Salter-Davies, R. D. (Chair), **The Problems of Youth Work in Rural Areas: A report of a working group set up by the Department of Education and Science on the recommendation of the Youth Service Development Council**, Department of Education and Science, 1969

81 Scott, Jackie, **Share and Chair Alike**, *Youth Service Scene*, no. 110, May 1985, pp6–7

82 Shanks, Kenneth, **Road Works: Mobile provision for youth**, National Playbus Association, 1992

83 Shropshire County Youth Service, **Social Education Needs of Rural Youth in Shropshire: First review and monitoring report August 1990**, Shropshire County Youth Service, 1990

84 Shropshire Youth Service, **Report on Work in Each Project of the Youth Service Northern Area**, Shropshire County Council, 1993

85 Shropshire Youth Service, **Report on Work in Each Project of the Youth Service Southern Area**, Shropshire County Council, 1993

86 Silverlock, Marion, **'Youth Work on Exmoor'**, *Youth in Society*, no. 112, March 1986, pp14–16

87 Somerset County Council Education Department, **Third National Rural Youth Work Conference Report**, Somerset County Council Education Department, 1987

88 Stern, Elliot and Turbin, Jill, **Youth Employment and Unemployment in Rural England: Report of the one-year pilot study in four rural areas for the Development Commission,** The Development Commission, 1986

89 Suffolk County Council Education Department, **Work with Young People in Rural Areas Policy Document**, Suffolk County Council Education Department, 1993

90 Thompson, Alan, Chairman, **Experience and Participation: Report of the review group on the youth service in England**, HMSO, 1982

91 Tyler, Mary, **'Ripe for Development'**, *Youth in Society*, no. 132, November 1987, pp10–12

92 Tyler, Mary, **'Youth Work in Cornwall'**, *Youth Service Scene*, no. 141, March 1988, pp6–7

93 Various, **'Working in Rural Settings'** (special issue), *Working with Girls*, no. 23, September–October 1984

94 Various, **Rural Youth Work**, National Youth Bureau, 1985

95 Walker, Catherine, **Across the Country: Developments in rural youth work**, National Youth Bureau, 1987

96 Wallace, Claire, Dunkley, David and Cheal, Brian, **'Young People in Rural South West England'**, *Youth and Policy*, no. 33, May 1991, pp10–16

97 Watson, Janet et al, **Rural Youth Work in Nottinghamshire**, Nottinghamshire County Council Leisure Services, Youth and Community Service, 1992

98 West Yorkshire Youth Association/ Humberside Youth Association, **Youth Work into the '90s: A review of year three September 1989–August 1990**, West Yorkshire Youth Association/ Humberside Youth Association, 1990

99 White, Peter, **Working with Rural Youth: Six case studies**, Youth Work Press, 1991

100 Wiggin, Mark, **Jigsaw Youth Integration Project Report 1992**, Trinity Youth and Community Centre, 1992

101 Wiltshire County Council Education Department, **Rural Strategy for Wiltshire Topic Paper Education: Youth and community services**, Wiltshire County Council Education Department, 1989

102 Working Party on Rural Youth Work, **Growing Up in a Rural Area: A reponse to the needs of young people in North Yorkshire**, North Yorkshire County Council Education Department County Youth Services, 1989

103 Wyre District Youth Service, **Report and Recommendations of the Preesall/ Knott End Research Project October 1987–March 1988**, Wyre District Youth Service, 1988

Appendix II

Key Rural Support Organisations

● **Action with Communities in Rural England (ACRE)**

ACRE is the collective voice and representative organisation for Rural Community Councils (RCCs) in England, and coordinates their views on various matters, including grant aid for the Rural Development Commission (RDC) and other funding bodies. ACRE provides training, management and fundraising advice for Rural Community Councils as well as a comprehensive advice and information service about rural areas.

Through its member RCCs, ACRE has a base in every rural county. The RCCs in turn are in touch with 11,000 parish councils, almost 9,000 village halls and many schools, youth groups, women's institutes and local voluntary organisations. ACRE also liaises with other rural agencies in Britain and Europe to share ideas and work together. It publishes an informative magazine entitled *Rural Viewpoint*.

• *Further information from ACRE, Somerford Court, Somerford Road, Cirencester, Gloucestershire GL7 1TW. Tel: 0285.653477.*

● **National Youth Agency (NYA)**

The NYA provides information and support for all those concerned with the informal and social education of young people. Funded primarily by central government (Department for Education, Voluntary Services Unit of the Home Office), it aims to provide a national focus for the youth service, both statutory and voluntary, and for all those who work with young people in the community, providing curriculum materials, organisational and management development, endorsement and accreditation of training, advice and support in the development of training, and a full range of information and publishing services.

The NYA's information centre contains a collection of books and reports on rural youth work which can be borrowed. A reading list on rural youth work and a briefing paper on sources of funding for youth work in rural areas – *Rural Initiatives* – is available for a small charge.

• *Further information from the National Youth Agency, 17–23 Albion Street, Leicester LE1 6GD. Tel/minicom: 0533.471200. Fax: 0533.471043.*

● **Rural Development Commission (RDC)**

The RDC advises the Government on economic and social matters affecting the rural areas of England and actively assists in their development. Its prime aim is to stimulate a wide range of job opportunities and the provision of essential services in the countryside.

In addition to national demonstration projects funded through the Rural Social Partnership Fund, the Commission supports rural voluntary action nationally through grants to ACRE and the National Council for Voluntary Youth Organisations. Support is given for local action through the RCCs and a wide range of projects targeted at areas and groups in greater need. It also provides assistance to facilitate the provision of affordable housing and transport.

Rural Social Partnership Fund

The Rural Social Partnership Fund is intended to support projects by non-statutory organisations at both national and local level. The Commission is interested in projects that:

♦ improve the understanding of disadvantage among particular groups in rural communities;

♦ demonstrate new ways of tackling the problems and meeting the needs which, if successful, can serve as a model for use more widely;

♦ disseminate good practice and successful innovation;

♦ enable specialist agencies to extend their activities into rural areas or widen their existing coverage within rural areas; and

♦ bring together in partnership bodies with an interest, an expertise or a responsibility for the delivery of services at national or local level.

Projects are expected to be aimed at people at a disadvantage in the following groups: children and young people; elderly people; those with mental or physical disabilities; women – particularly mothers with young children or those seeking to return to work; people caring for relatives and friends; the unemployed and others on low incomes.

In addition to the direct costs of projects, grants may also be given for research, monitoring and evaluation, publications and dissemination. Financial support is limited to a maximum of three years. Grants will not normally exceed 50 per cent of the total cost of the project and the maximum grant in any one financial year will be £50,000 per project.

Local Projects

Local youth projects may be eligible for grant aid from the Commission under other funding headings. These will be administered through RDC area offices who should be contacted for further details. Projects such as mobile youth buses have been funded from this source in the past.

• *For information and advice on the services provided by the RDC and details of the network of regional RDC offices contact the Rural Development Commission, 141 Castle Street, Salisbury, Wiltshire SP1 3PT. Tel: 0722.336255.*

• *Administrative headquarters for the RDC are at 17–19 Dacre Street, London SW1H 0DH. Tel: 071.340.2900. Fax: 071.340.2911.*

● **Rural Enterprise Information Service (REIS)**

REIS is a service provided by the National Rural Enterprise Centre based at Stoneleigh in Warwickshire. It was launched in July 1989. The information held by REIS is summarised information for practitioners on who is doing what, where, when and how on issues relevant to rural economic development in the UK. Supporting information is also held or accessed as required. Features of the service include:

♦ agencies – a new comprehensive database of over three thousand agencies relevant to the rural economy;

♦ initiatives – a new database holding, at present, over three hundred current or very recent initiatives;

- library – key books, journals and papers;
- key geographical information on activities by county and district, with geographical searches available for all the databases; and
- funds – information on key business and economic indicators which is intended to develop into a market intelligence service.

The National Rural Enterprise Centre has become a focus for research, development projects, information and seminars in the rural sector, both in the UK and the EEC. The subscriber network includes over a hundred and forty organisations from all parts of the UK and from the EEC. Agencies include national and local government, enterprise agencies, and a wide range of voluntary and statutory bodies. By subscribing to REIS, organisations or individuals have access to the business, agricultural, local authority and voluntary sector network, and the sharing of practical development experience that occurs at the National Agricultural Centre.
• *Further information from Ruth King, Information Officer, National Rural Enterprise Centre, National Agricultural Centre, Stoneleigh, Warwickshire CV8 2LZ. Tel: 0203.696765.*

● **Rural Impetus**
Campaigning group of rural youth work practitioners aiming to advance the cause of youth work with young people in rural areas throughout the country. Newsletter, *Rural Impetus*, produced on a regular basis.
• *Further information from Ray Fabes, School of Applied Social Sciences, De Montfort University, Scraptoft Campus, Scraptoft, Leicester LE7 9SU. Tel: 0533.577743.*

● **Rural Team/National Council for Voluntary Organisations (NCVO)**
The NCVO is committed to a rural dimension across its whole organisation. The Rural Team exists to promote this and, more broadly, to support rural voluntary action throughout the country. The team focuses on the generic issues facing voluntary organisations working in rural areas – for example, the high costs and low levels of funding – and on enabling other organisations to develop their rural work. The team convenes a regular meeting of workers from national rural development projects, and contributes briefings on rural issues to *NCVO News*.
• *Further information from NCVO, Rural Team, Regent's Wharf, 8 All Saints Street, London N1 9RL. Tel: 071.713.6161.*

● **Rural Youth Work Network**
Forum of rural youth work practitioners, supported by the NYA, meeting twice a year to share practice, discuss issues and act as a collaborative voice where necessary.
• *Further information from Youth Work Development Section, National Youth Agency, 17–23 Albion Street, Leicester LE1 6GD. Tel/minicom: 0533.471200. Fax: 0533.471043.*

● **Youth Clubs UK**
Rural Links Project – a three-year project, part funded by the RDC started in November 1993 which focuses on the training of voluntary managers and workers, working with young people aged 8 to 14 living in rural areas. The target groups are the 27 local youth associations which fall within the RDC priority areas.
• *Further information from Kris Felton, Bryony Cottage, Church Lane, Longworth, Oxford OX13 5DX. Tel: 071.353.2366 (Youth Clubs UK).*

Appendix III

Significant Dates in Rural Youth Work

1944 Publication of *A Rural Youth Service: Suggestions for youth work in the countryside* by Désirée Edwards-Rees

1946 Publication of *Youth and the Village Club* by Edith M. Clark

1963 Youth Service Development Council Subcommittee report *The Problems of Youth Work in Rural Areas* by R. D. Salter-Davis

1978 Formation of Campaign for Rural Youth (CRY)

1979 Publication of paper *Missed the Bus* on rural youth work issues by CRY

Establishment of Rural Youth Work Education Project by the National Association of Youth Clubs

1982 Thompson Report *Experience and Participation: Report of the review group on the youth service in England* devotes five paragraphs to youth work in rural areas

1983 Publication of *Groundwork: Young people and the youth service in the countryside* by

Michael Akehurst, director of NAYC Rural Youth Work Education Project

1984 National Association of Youth Clubs publishes *Fieldwork: An aid to the support of youth workers* by Michael Akehurst

National Youth Bureau (NYB) publishes *Shadows of Adolescence: Images from West Dorset* by Allan Kennedy

1985 First National Symposium on Rural Youth Work in Buckinghamshire from 10–12 September

Rural Youth Work – series of articles from *Youth in Society*

1986 Formation of Rural Impetus Group

NACYS Rural Youth Work Subcommittee established

Second National Symposium on Rural Youth Work held at Borwick Hall, Lancashire from 22–24 September

1987 Formation of the Rural Youth Work Network, convened by NYB

Third National Symposium on Rural Youth Work in Somerset from 30 September to 2 October

1988 Publication by the DES of the National Advisory Council for the Youth Service (NACYS) report *Youth Work in Rural Areas*

1990 National Association of Youth and Community Education Officers (NAYCEO) policy paper on youth work in rural areas

Approval of three-year youth work in rural areas project based at NYB funded by the RDC

Training event, Innovations in Rural Practice, held from 3–5 October in London

Second Ministerial Conference on the Youth Service held in Birmingham from 7–8 November which reached agreement on a Statement of Purpose, priorities, outcomes, provision and

performance indicators for youth work

1991 Lessons from Contemporary Practice – policy event on rural youth work on 9 October aboard HMS President, London

1992 Third Ministerial Conference for the Youth Service held in Blackpool from 15–16 June which included a workshop presentation from the Rural Youth Work Network

1993 Completion of the NYA/RDC project on rural youth work

Start of the part-RDC funded Rural Link Project based at Youth Clubs UK providing training for workers with 8 to 14-year-old children and young people

1994 NYA publishes *Youth Work in Rural Areas: A training pack*

Nothing Ever Happens Around Here: Developing work with young people in rural areas published by NYA

Appendix IV

The RDC Project Reference Group Membership

Peter Ali
regional development worker for the Crusaders in East Anglia

Ian Bell
district team leader (youth work), Cumbria LEA

Nicky Davey
youth worker – participation project, Youth Clubs Cornwall

Ray Fabes
senior lecturer, Leicester Polytechnic/ De Montfort University

Roger Kingston
rural outreach worker, East Sussex County Council

David Popham
part-time youth worker – rural villages project, Leicester diocese

Diana Power
development worker, Scoutreach project, Lincolnshire

David Schweizer
voluntary youth service support officer – Avon County Council, community leisure department

Helen Thomson
Rural Development Commission

Elfride Vaughan
area youth worker – Wincanton, Somerset

Hazel Wallis
until 1991 centre-based rural youth worker, Hereford and Worcester

Sandra Wood
until 1992 county rural youth officer, Hertfordshire LEA/YFC

ABOUT THE PUBLISHER

The National Youth Agency provides information and support for all those concerned with the informal and social education of young people. Funded primarily by central government*, it aims to provide a national focus for the youth service, both statutory and voluntary, and for all those who work with young people in the community, providing curriculum materials, organisational and management development, endorsement and accreditation of training, advice and support in the development of training, and a full range of information and publishing services.

The NYA is also the major impetus behind the Information Shops initiative, which offers high-quality high-street information provision to young people.

*Department for Education, Voluntary Services Unit of the Home Office